Images of War
Rommel in North Africa:
Quest for the Nile

David Mitchelhill-Green

Pen & Sword
MILITARY

First published in Great Britain in 2017 by
PEN & SWORD MILITARY
an imprint of
Pen & Sword Books Ltd,
47 Church Street,
Barnsley,
South Yorkshire.
S70 2AS

Copyright © David Mitchelhill-Green, 2017

A CIP record for this book is available from the British Library.

ISBN 9781473892200

Printed and bound in England
By CPI Group (UK) Ltd, Croydon, CR0 4YY

Pen & Sword Books Ltd incorporates the Imprints of
Pen & Sword Aviation, Pen & Sword Maritime,
Pen & Sword Military, Wharncliffe Local History, Pen & Sword Select,
Pen & Sword Military Classics and Leo Cooper.

For a complete list of Pen & Sword titles please contact
Pen & Sword Books Limited
47 Church Street, Barnsley, South Yorkshire, S70 2AS, England
E-mail: enquiries@pen-and-sword.co.uk
Website: www.pen-and-sword.co.uk

Contents

Acknowledgments

My sincere appreciation is extended to the following individuals and their collective expertise who helped make this book possible: Bertram Nold, Francisco de Asís Romero Medina, Bob Johnston, Fausto Corsetti, Bill Murray, Pierce Fox and Dr Petra Bopp.

Many thanks also to the enthusiastic staff of Pen & Sword: Roni and Paul Wilkinson, Matt Jones and Barnaby Blacker.

This book is dedicated to Hana & Harvey Mitchelhill.

Abbreviations, Conventions and Definitions

Aufklärungsgruppe	reconnaissance group
ADC	aide-de-camp
AP	armour-piercing
Ausführung/Ausf	model/type
Balkenkreuz	straight-armed cross symbol of the Wehrmacht
Befehlswagen	command tank
Beute	booty, spoils
Beutefahrzeuge	captured vehicles
bhp	brake horsepower
CMP	Canadian Military Pattern
Corpo di Spedizione Italiano	Italian Expeditionary Corps in Russia
DAK	*Deutsches Afrikakorps* (German Africa Corps)
DAF	British Desert Air Force
Flak	*Flugzeugabwehrkanone* or anti-aircraft gun
Heer	German Army
HE	high explosive
Jagdgeschwader	fighter squadron
Kleiner Panzerbefehlswagen	small command tank
Kraftradfahrer	motorcyclist
Kriegsmarine	German Navy
Kriegsberichterstatter	war correspondent
Leichter Funkpanzerwagen	light radio armoured vehicle
Leichter Panzerspähwagen	light reconnaissance armoured car
Luftwaffe	German Air Force
OKW	*Oberkommando der Wehrmacht* (the Supreme Armed Forces Command)
Pak	*Panzerabwehrkanone* or anti-tank gun
Panzerjäger	'tank hunter'
Panzerkampfwagen	tank, literally 'armoured fighting vehicle', abbreviated as Pz.Kpfw. or Panzer

Panzerjäger Abteilung	'tank hunting battalion'
RAF	Royal Air Force
Regio Esercito	Royal Italian Army
Reichs-Rundfunk-Gesellschaft	Reich Broadcasting Corporation
Reichspropagandaminister	Minister of Propaganda
Schwere Feldhaubitze	heavy field howitzer
Schwere Panzerspähwagen	heavy reconnaissance armoured car
Sonderführer	'specialist leader' such as interpreters, propaganda officials
Sonderkraftfahrzeug	'special-purpose vehicle', an ordnance number, abbreviated as 'Sd.Kfz.'
Sperrverband	'blocking force'
Stabsstaffel	'staff squadron'
Stuka	*Sturzkampfflugzeug* ('dive bomber')
Verbandskennzeichen	operational code
Vormarsch	'advance'
Wehrmacht	German Armed Forces
Wehrmacht-Rundfunkempfänger	Wehrmacht broadcast receiver
Zerstörergeschwader	'destroyer wing'

Notes on Photography and Sources

The majority of the photographs used in this book were drawn from the US National Archives and Records Administration (NARA). Taken by various German and Italian photographers, it is possible that Rommel, a keen photographer, also took some. As a record of the North African campaign, the photographs in this book, not surprisingly, present the Desert War through a relatively narrow lens. They portray a sense of camaraderie within the coalition desert force; the desertscape appears flat and devoid of sandstorms or the flooding rains that could quickly turn the dusty surface into a quagmire. No evidence is seen of the fly problem, a plague 'worse than the heat' as Rommel's adjutant Hans-Joachim Schraepler penned. The range of clothing worn, from shorts to greatcoats, is testament to the extremes in temperature. The Axis' reliance on captured British vehicles, in this highly mobile arena, is evident, intimating the long distances covered, the insufficiency of Axis vehicles and the high breakdown rate of vehicles designed for European conditions. Benito Mussolini's inability to wage war against a modern adversary is evident in the elderly mix of artillery fielded by the Italians; Rommel's chronic logistical headache is glimpsed through the shots of an Italian submarine visiting Bardia to deliver supplies; and we observe Rommel in his prime as the 'Desert Fox', an ambitious general intent on reaching the Nile.

Note that place names, in keeping with the period, have been retained in the form common at the time.

Rommel pictured with his Leica camera, a gift from Joseph Goebbels. An ardent photographer, he often requested that his ADC take a shot that included him. During the French campaign he wrote to his wife, Lucie, requesting that she 'cut out all the newspaper articles' featuring him. Later during the evening of 7 February 1941, he penned a 'coded' letter to her explaining that his new assignment would hasten his 'rheumatism treatment', his physician having recommended the warm North African climate as a remedy for his condition.

Introduction

Rommel, Rommel, Rommel! Does anything else count except beating him?' an exasperated Winston Churchill vented in an incident later quoted in his memoirs. Noting the importance Britain's military leadership was placing on Rommel, Adolf Hitler remarked how they were 'able to explain their defeat to their nation more easily by focusing on Rommel.' Several days later Germany's Führer cited Churchill's speeches in the House of Commons which, 'for political reasons', 'repeatedly presented [Rommel] as a general with genius-like capabilities.' Hitler also questioned whether such praise was designed to 'foster discord between the Italians and us by emphasising Rommel…Consequently he has acknowledged Rommel's achievements many times to the world…This fact shows how dangerous it is to put so much emphasis on a capable opponent's man as Churchill has done in the case of Rommel. A name suddenly begins to acquire a meaning this way that is equal in value to several divisions.' To this end Erwin Rommel achieved the extraordinary feat of becoming a legend – on both sides – during his own lifetime. Today he remains the most well-known German general of the Second World War.

   To gain a deeper understanding of Rommel's character and the merits of his leadership in North Africa, we begin with a series of firsthand accounts written by officers who served with him in the desert, a theme continued throughout the book. Rather than a chronological retelling of the fighting across Libya and Egypt, this work is a pictorial examination of Rommel's quest to reach the Nile during 1941-42. We start with a post-war report by Rainer Karl-Theodore Kriebel, former *Deutsches Afrikakorps* (DAK) staff officer, written for US military intelligence: 'In the year 1941 the African Desert was a new world not only for the German Command and the German troops. Desert warfare as a form of fighting was something new for the entire modern science of war. It was found that the desert offered undreamt-of possibilities for the decisive weapons of modern war, viz. the armour and the air force. On the African war theatre more than on other theatres of war, modern command methods found all the scope to show what could be done. In other directions too, the African campaign is of particular interest. For the first time the Axis powers were faced by the problems of a confederate war. For the student of military history, the African campaign offers fascinating themes such as General Rommel's leadership and how he had been able to develop into a leading personality of first class order, a personality soaring to ever greater heights of achievement as the tasks grew more formidable and his experience – dearly bought – grew richer. For the German rank and file, it is particularly the first year of the African campaign which will be unforgettable. In no other theatre did the superb soldierly qualities of the German fighting troops show up so brilliantly as in Africa. Separated from home by thousands of kilometres, cut off from any reinforcements and supplies for months by huge stretches of ocean ruled by the enemy, the German soldier has done his duty without fail and has adapted himself in a surprisingly short time to the unusual and difficult conditions of climate and terrain. But justice demands that the achievements of the Italian armed forces do not go without recognition; they have done their very best in conditions much less favourable and equipped with inferior materials, never have they fought more valiantly than under Rommel's leadership. These qualities of the German and the Italian soldier had the opportunities to show themselves in a brilliant way because in the North African campaign they found a brave and fair enemy in the British soldier. In this century of soulless mass warfare, the African campaign stands out as an uplifting exception where two chivalrous opponents borne by mutual respect fought decently and cleanly.

Writing after the war, *Generalleutnant* Alfred Gause wrote of Rommel's command techniques and eventual defeat in Africa: 'The conditions of the African theatre enabled Rommel to employ methods different from those he would have had to employ in Europe in commanding an army flanked by other units and under some superior command. In Africa he was completely independent in his conduct of operations. His next superior, the Governor General of Libya, was usually hundreds of miles distant, and most of the time no telephone communications existed. Directives concerning the conduct of operations arrived only rarely and then were usually in accordance with his own recommendations. Whenever his opinion on matters of fundamental importance differed from that held at higher headquarters, he succeeded in having his way. As Kesselring complains: "Neither discussions nor orders could influence Rommel." In the absence of rearward telephone lines, no telephone messages requiring sudden decisions were to be expected and Rommel therefore in his command placed main emphasis on his own mobility. Leaving the forward echelon of his army headquarters staff in an established command post, Rommel established himself and a very small staff, which usually included me and a number of messenger officers, on vehicles…For his own protection Rommel took along only two armoured reconnaissance cars, and it must be remembered that he was usually in the foremost lines, sometimes even further ahead, and sometimes in the area on the open flank. This small staff was always on the move and it was from here that Rommel conducted operations. Radio messages were sent and received frequently while in movement. Since Rommel as a matter of principle directed operations personally from the area of main effort and based his decisions on his own observations, no time was lost in waiting for reports.

'It must be admitted that that the method described here was inconvenient for some subordinate commanders because Rommel used to interfere in the control of individual units if he thought it necessary. On the other hand, however, he also accepted exclusive responsibility for all tactical and strategic action taken. Basic decisions on the field of battle he left to no other person. Every unit commander and every man knew that in the most difficult situations, and no matter how heavy the fire was, Rommel would appear in person and would master the situation. He never allowed any slack in the reins of control. Nobody ever had the feeling that he was forsaken. It was in this way that his indefinable sway developed, which also influenced the enemy, and which enabled him even after serious reverses to maintain the morale and spirit of the troops, evidenced by his recapture of the Cyrenaica in February 1942 although he had received no reinforcements after his difficult winter retreat. In this case of his retreat from El Alamein to Tunisia the morale of the approximately 70,000 troops involved remained unimpaired.

'As Mussolini put it: "Your withdrawal was a masterpiece, Field Marshal." These methods of command presuppose a robust constitution, disdain for personal safety, and an almost ascetic frugality. During operations Rommel slept only a few hours each day out in the desert, without any tent or trailer, and ate only cold food without even leaving his car for meals. No cooking utensils were taken along. ... While conducting operations in this highly flexible and mobile manner Rommel at no time lost sight of the overall situation, in spite of being away from his established command post. He was kept currently informed by means of brief radio messages and did not base his decisions exclusively on fleeting local impressions.

'In consonance with the principles generally valid in the German Armed Forces, Rommel conducted operations with extreme dash and free from any stereotype rules. To retain the initiative was one of the cardinal laws. The general strength ratios and the supply situation compelled him to always attack numerically stronger forces...'

Against the Bir Hacheim/Gazala line in 1942: 'Determination and flexibility of command had to compensate for what was lacking in matériel. He could not afford to attempt to break through the heavily mined British positions, because he lacked the necessary tanks and ammunition for this purpose. His decision to outflank the positions in the south was a grave risk, particularly since all supplies had to be moved forward around the British flank. Defeat in this battle might have involved the loss of Africa. However, Rommel was compelled to attack in order to anticipate offensive action by the British Eighth Army and retain the initiative.

'In all operations he was compelled to employ his numerically inferior forces in tight concentration in order at least to achieve a certain measure of local superiority in the area of the main effort. He was called the "Master in the Art of Poor-Man Warfare." Any single reverse could have resulted in a complete catastrophe, and the whole situation in Libya hinged upon the Panzer Army. There could be no hope in a crisis of speedily receiving reinforcements by sea.

'In spite of his boldness Rommel was not rash. While requiring the utmost personal effort from himself and from every officer and man under his command, he at no time made excessive demands on his troops. His constant close contact with the troops on combat enabled him to recognise in time not only the limits of the units in action but also of the entire army and of the entire military potential available in Northern Africa.

'The question of whether Rommel's command methods were sound must be answered in the affirmative so far as Africa was concerned. They are vindicated by his successes…In Africa Rommel developed his methods of command unrestrictedly in consonance with his nature. These methods would be difficult to teach and can hardly be applied under general circumstances. In spite of uniform training every commander develops his own particular methods consonant with his mentality.

'The campaign in Africa required exceptionally strong nerves to weather the numerous crises which developed. Rommel believed in his good fortune but it did not allow local successes to mislead or failures to discourage him. The fate of Northern Africa hinged upon him personally and when the British Eighth Army launched its attack in October 1942 he had to leave Semering, where he was under medical treatment, in order to resume command over his army, although his health was not yet fully restored.

'What was the basis of Rommel's influence over his troops? Fundamentally, Rommel was hard, uncompromising, and impersonal. He judged persons solely by their performances and sought favour neither with his superiors not with those subordinate to him…His maxim was that the best way to take care of the troops was to give them the best possible training. What earned him the respect, devotion and loyalty of his troops was his personal courage and his absolute reliability in the conduct of operations. His men were proud and had blind confidence in him.

'In spite of the performances and sacrifices he extracted from them. Rommel felt personally responsible for each and every individual serving under him and demanded this same attitude in his sub-commanders in their attitude towards their troops. Any unit commander who failed to measure up to his high standards in this respect was relieved of his command immediately and returned to the zone of the Interior.

'The loss of Africa was not due to any failure of Rommel as a commander, to his failing nerves or health (he mastered bouts of ill health by energy), or to his "pessimism", as some people chose to describe his assessment of the situation based on realistic estimates, but to the overwhelming numerical superiority of the forces put into the field from Egypt and in French Northern Africa by the Western Allies against the seriously depleted Axis forces. However, the command authorities in Europe failed to realise this fact.

'If he had been allowed to use his own judgment he would have succeeded, as he stated literally to the present writer, in withdrawing the bulk of his forces to Europe in time. Then, if he had been allowed a free hand, he would have been able at least to offer more tenacious resistance against an Allied attack against Sicily and Italy, which he considered as a logical follow-up of the invasion of Northern Africa. Because he was not allowed to take such appropriate action, events in Africa took their logical military course as predicted repeatedly and urgently by Rommel well ahead of time.'

Wrote Siegfried Westphal, 'As far as his military capabilities were concerned, Rommel was often ironically called the "Feldherr of the extreme front line". By this was meant that the command of an army was too high a promotion for him, who had not passed through the refining school of the General Staff. It is true that he made serious mistakes, as witness his premature attempt to cut off the enemy retreat in November 1941, and his advance to Alamein after the fall of Tobruk. But the overwhelming majority of his actions testify to an uncommon tactical ability and a general military capacity far above the average. All who worked with him were constantly astounded at the rapidity which he summed up the most complex situations and came to the heart of the matter.'

German war correspondent Hans Gert Freiherr von Esebeck recalled in 1944

Rommel's rapport with his frontline troops: '...we find him everywhere, and always there is this strange magic strength that this soldier radiates to his troops, right down to the last rifleman. The privates call him "Erwin" – just that: "Erwin", short and to the point. Not that they intend any disrespect by using his christian name – it is a mark of profound admiration. Because the men can understand their commander-in-chief: when he talks with them he calls a spade a spade; he doesn't sentimentalize with them, but meets them as man to man, often uses hard language at them but also knows how to praise and encourage them and make suggestions and make complicated subjects easily comprehensible to them. Of course to start with there were few of us – everybody else knew everybody else and there was a desert camaraderie: the rifleman saw his general eating the same classical Libyan diet of sardines.'

Rommel, according to Friedrich von Mellenthin, DAK staff officer, 'was the logical commander for desert warfare. His main strength, the immediate command of forces right on the battlefield, could be given full play in such broad, open spaces. Army field orders which failed to keep pace with the developing situation could, therefore, be given bold, rapid, and flexible revision on the spot by a direct order from Rommel...it may be said that Rommel was a commander blessed with a special talent for leading mobile forces in desert warfare.' His 'custom of "leading from the front" occasionally told against him; decisions affecting the army as a whole were sometimes influenced unduly by purely local successes or failures. On the other hand by going himself to the danger spot–and he had an uncanny faculty for appearing at the right place at the right time – he was able to adapt his plans to new situations and in the fluid conditions of the Western Desert this was a factor of supreme importance.'

We must remember, however, that much of Rommel's *Fingerspitzengefühl* (or 'fingertip feel') for the battlefield was due to the work of his intelligence sources, in particular the outstanding work of his *Nachrichten Fern Aufklärung Kompanie* 621 (Signals Intercept Company 621), which provided remarkable tactical insights from the intercepted British radio transmissions. The decoding of detailed communiqués from the American military attaché in Cairo, Colonel Bonner F. Fellers, were also, according to Rommel's former intelligence officer, Hans-Otto Behrendt, 'stupefying' in their 'openness'. Access to Fellers' detailed reports proved spectacularly useful in the weeks after 26 May 1942 when Axis forces punched through the Gazala Line and captured Tobruk. Rommel's 'tactical feel' was never as pronounced after the two intelligence sources stopped by early July 1942.

In Berlin, General Franz Halder, Chief of the General Staff, noted in July 1941 that Rommel's 'character defects make him extremely hard to get along with, but no one cares to come out in open opposition because of his brutality and the backing he has on top level.' Stressing the value of frontline leadership – 'the commander must go up to see for himself; reports received second-hand rarely give the information he needs for his decisions' – Rommel was often absent from his headquarters for extended periods, much to the frustration of his chiefs of staff, who were often unaware of his exact position. Moreover, his habit of giving orders to the person on the spot, or changing plans impulsively to meet new circumstances, was a 'real thorn in the flesh' for his subordinate commanders, who 'resented it bitterly'.

While Oberleutnant Harald Kuhn (5th Panzer Regiment) wrote favourably of Rommel's 'personal courage, his energy level, his imagination' and 'military good fortune', he also highlighted his 'need to be in control, his ambition and the ruthlessness with which he brought those qualities to bear. The self-indulgence of that type of personality also brings great danger with it. If it does not suceed in establishing a basis of trust between it and its surroundings, it becomes all too easily arrogant, impatient, distrustful, unjust and – lonely…whenever we saw and heard that Rommel preferred to be far to the front on days of combat in order to direct individual tanks and assault detachments, instead of making decisions in his headquarters, which the overall situation demanded, or when he again demonstrated that he had completely underestimated or incorrectly estimated the enemy, then we asked ourselves whether he was really such a great military leader.'

Regarding Rommel's habit of interfering at the front, Rainer Kriebel felt that the conduct of operations had suffered, in November 1941, '…because Rommel had not clearly defined the sphere of command of the DAK, and often interfered personally in the command of particular units, without informing the division in question or the DAK. A number of mutually contradictory orders was the result. In the end the divisions took matters into their own hands simply by acting on their own initiative without reference to orders, as the situation required. Frequently the orders given by Rommel on the spot contradicted every tactical principle and resulted in expensive failure. For instance, tanks were repeatedly sent in to attack well-mined field fortifications with no support from other weapons….'

In relation to Rommel's rapport with his Italian ally, Generalmajor Burkhart Müller-Hillebrand held that his 'exceptionally strong personality often exceeded his authority.

It must be admitted, however, that German and Italian views on tactics diverged very considerably, that the two forces differed greatly in the quality of their equipment, and that the Italian troops, due to their earlier defeats, were shaken and demoralised. Since full utilisation of the high qualities of the German forces would not have taken place if they had been completely subordinate and made to operate in close collaboration with the Italian forces, a deviation from the principle of unified command authority may well have been justified in this case. During the campaign in Africa, which unquestionably was an Italian campaign, the German command paid less and less attention to its nominal subordination to the superior Italian commander. There was also an increasing tendency to combine units of the two nations and at times even the staffs were composed of both Italians and Germans.'

The *Regio Esercito*, it must be remembered, struggled under inferior leadership, mediocre training and, as will be seen, generally obsolete weaponry. A harsh critic of his ally, Rommel's opinion tended to alter with changing fortunes. 'There can be no disputing that the achievements of all the Italian units, especially the motorised elements, far outstripped any action of the Italian Army for 100 years,' he wrote in his memoirs about the summer battles of 1942. 'Many Italian generals and officers won our admiration both as men and soldiers.' Reiner Kriebel believed that the blame often accorded to the Italians did not do justice to the efforts of their troops: 'It must be stated that the commands of the Italian Corps and the Italian divisions during the fighting around Tobruk and the following withdrawal [in late 1941] and its battles fully understood the importance of holding out, and they did their utmost to fulfil the tasks Rommel had allotted to them. The Italian soldier was enthusiastic, moderate in his demands and of a persevering nature. His southlandish nature, however, brought it about that he easily panicked when the situation became critical. He was more easily impressed and depressed by setbacks than his German comrade-in-arms. In most cases his training left much to be desired, which resulted in correspondingly higher losses. For years the Italian soldiers had not been relieved nor given leave; they were insufficiently fed and they were underpaid; thus their physical and psychological power of resistance naturally weakened in the course of the campaign. They felt very bitter about their inferior equipment and armament. In this connection the small range of the obsolete system of laying their guns deserves particular mention. On many occasions Italian guns were shot to pieces by British batteries at long range before they could even open fire. The calibre of the Italian anti-tank guns was insufficient; the Italian tanks were insufficiently armoured and armed; the Italian anti-aircraft artillery was obsolete. It is therefore not surprising that the Italian troops felt that they were inferior to the British. Nonetheless individual Italian units have achieved good results and some of them have fought to the bitter end. Such individual cases do, however, not change the general picture as it presents itself when seen against the background of the prevailing circumstances.'

What of Rommel's British adversaries? Albert Kesselring, Luftwaffe Generalfeldmarschall, recalled: 'I never quite understood the train of thought of the British command. Military history will have to decide whether the British were then pressing on in aimless pursuit, exploiting their dearly-bought initial success in the hope of beating Rommel decisively and thus winning all of Africa, or whether they had planned the entire operation as a well thought-out battle of annihilation. The wide open spaces of Africa are undoubtedly made to order for large-scale movements. The few roads and tracks as well as the limited passability of desert terrain in the North African Theatre of Operations constitute a definite disadvantage. In suitable places even minor forces can stop an attack by a superior enemy. In addition, the long distance involved, stretching partly across desert terrain, resulted in attrition of men and matériel.

'Many a mistake by the command, a certain slowness in arriving at decisions, an advance too methodical and an inclination to split up forces: all these things worked together in denying the British the expected results. On the other hand there was the unfailing will for victory, the hardness and stubbornness which must be admired and which never flagged even in situations which seemed to be hopeless. The courage of the British troops throughout the fighting has secured them the high esteem of their enemies. On the whole the achievements of the British troops and men, are on a high level.'

Reflecting on Rommel's triumph at the beginning of 1942, Rainer Kriebel believed that the 'measures taken by the British certainly contributed considerably to the success achieved. It is difficult to understand why, during January, the British Command split up their forces to such an extent and why they neglected to take the necessary defensive steps. General Rommel skilfully took advantage of these mistakes. He hit the British Eighth Army in the moment of its greatest weakness. British supplies were not yet arriving in sufficient quantities, because the port of Benghazi was not usable. Transport of supplies by land was not yet functioning smoothly, as the coastal road had only become available a few days back, after the Sollum positions had fallen. At the beginning of the counter-offensive Rommel once again proved himself a past master at concealing his intentions and deceiving the enemy. Thus the surprise sprung on the British Command was a complete success not only operationally but also tactically.'

Rommel's shortcomings as a commander ultimately condemned his army to defeat. Notwithstanding his tactical brilliance, a lack of staff training underscored an ignorance of the broader context of Hitler's war and the fact that the campaign in North Africa was fundamentally defensive. Moreover, a failure to comprehend the enormous supply needs of a mobile army in the desert rendered his audacious advances unsustainable. Concerning Rommel's logistical nightmare, Mellenthin understood that the 'quartermaster occupied a difficult position, for not until 1941-42, when reverses were suffered in this field, did Rommel give more attention to the supply situation. Typical of the importance which he placed on the supply problem is the following statement from Rommel: "We'll get our gasoline from the British".'

Defeated in Africa, Rommel was again beaten in Normandy following the D-Day landings in June 1944. Yet his fame in the English-speaking world continued to grow after the German surrender in May 1945 both as an accomplice in the 20 July 1944 plot to kill Hitler and as the chivalrous leader of the Afrikakorps. His posthumous renown during the Cold War was further fuelled by a sympathetic portrayal by James Mason in the 1951 motion picture and in the pages of several bestselling complimentary British post-war biographies. Rommel became the archetypal German officer irrespective of the Wehrmacht's subsequent implication in genocidal atrocities. As one contemporary reviewer observed, Rommel was 'the British Army's favourite German general'. Critics of the legend included Labour MP Richard Crossman, a former psychological warfare office, who argued: 'During the war we adopted Rommel, along with Lili Marlene, and made him an honorary Englishman by picturing him as the one German who played war according to the rules of cricket. Of course, this is a myth; many other German generals felt a distaste for the SS methods, and Rommel was by no stretch of the imagination a gentleman…As a nation, we deceive ourselves into believing that there are two sorts of Germans – Good Germans and Bad Germans. The "Bad Germans" are militarists, Nazis, anti-democratic, and perpetrators of atrocities. The "Good Germans" are peace-loving democrats and real gentlemen. Ergo, since Rommel was a clean fighter, he must have been anti-Nazi, and men like him make good allies of democracy against the Russians.'

Singling Rommel out as a 'good' German aided post-war rapprochement in the West as the likelihood of a new war with the Soviet Union escalated. Here was a figurehead for West Germany's newly established *Bundeswehr*, an army that would fight alongside other NATO nations in the event of a new conflict. The *Bundeswehr* even sent delegations to reunions of former Afrikakorps veterans, honouring Rommel as 'the most magnificent soldier and great man', a 'role model and obligation for us young soldiers'. Army barracks carried his name as did a new Bundesmarine Lütjens-class destroyer.

In a letter to Kirchheim in 1959, Johannes Streich (former commander of the 5th Light Division) expressed his opinion that 'thanks to propaganda, first by Goebbels, then by [Bernard] Montgomery, and finally, after he was poisoned, by all the former enemy powers, he has become a symbol of the best military traditions. His qualities of leadership are glorified, as are those of his character, especially his chivalry, generosity and humility …Any public criticism of this already legendary personality would damage the esteem in which the German soldier is held.'

However, few remember the labour camps – holding 2,500 Jews in Libya and 5,000 Jews in Tunisia – and the thousands of rural Tunisian Jews forced to wear the Star of David. Also forgotten are the reprisals and racial attacks against North African Jews, and the arrival of SS personnel in Tunisia in 1942.

More recent historiographical examinations have begun to unravel the 'Rommel myth', accepting in part his flair for tactical innovation, audacity and personal bravery, but also highlighting a disregard for logistical realities, a penchant for bypassing the chain of command in seeking direct access to Hitler and myopia toward to the Wehrmacht's broader strategy in 1941-42.

We finish with the words of one of Rommel's adversaries in the desert, General Sir John Hackett: 'Rommel may have been egotistical, vain, self-seeking, often unfair and sometimes no great respecter of the truth, someone in whose complex makeup the most wholly admirable single feature was his deep devotion to his wife [though Hackett was clearly unaware of Rommel's rumoured mistress, Walburga Stemmer and his illegitimate daughter, Gertrud, born on 8 December 1913]. His planning, if you could call it that, may have driven his supply staff to despair. There was clearly little sense in his abandonment of the battle still unresolved in Libya to take an armoured force in a swift dash toward the [Nile] Delta, only possible if he were to be able to pick up fuel in great abundance from supply dumps captured on the way. It is not easy to defend his conduct of operations in North Africa, pressing on at the farthest extent of a tenuous supply line, when it was clearly evident that the fuel and ammunition most urgently required could not be got to him across the Mediterranean at the rate of loss then being inflicted by the British. On the other hand, though he had many enemies, he could inspire troops to follow him to a degree few have equalled. He was bold, imaginative, and brave, with a tactical sense at times approaching genius. His method of command was forceful, direct, and personal. If he wanted something done, he was there to get it done and he was harsh on those he thought had failed him. There was no better commander of armoured troops in a fluid battle, on either side in any theatre of the war and no one was more willingly followed by his troops. They understood him as thoroughly as he understood them. He led, as all good leaders do, from the inside.'

This is the story of Erwin Rommel in North Africa and his quest for the Nile.

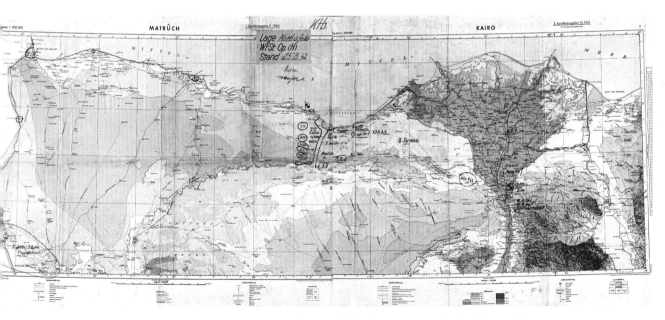

German situation map of North Africa dated 26 August 1942, Cairo and the Nile Delta visible to the right of the British 8th Army.

Chapter One
Hitler's Sunflower

At a meeting at his Bavarian alpine retreat, the Berghof, on 8 and 9 January 1941, Adolf Hitler announced that an armoured 'blocking force' would be transported to Libya on 22 February. German involvement in North Africa was formally sanctioned in his Directive No. 22, dated 11 January 1941: 'The situation in the Mediterranean area, where England is employing superior forces against our allies, requires that Germany should assist for reasons of strategy, politics, and psychology.' The operation was code-named *Sonnenblume* (Sunflower).

One of the first Pz.Kpfw. III to arrive in North Africa.

Panzer crew in continental uniforms help unload a Pz.Kpfw. I *Ausführung* A (Sd.Kfz. 101). This 5.4-ton light tank with a crew of two was produced from 1934 to 1936. Progressively withdrawn from frontline combat in 1940, the obsolete vehicle last saw service in Finland and North Africa in 1941. Prone to overheating and engine breakdowns, it was soon withdrawn from action and cannibalized to provide spare parts for the *Panzerjäger* 1s of the *Panzerjäger Abteilung* 605.

The Roman 'I' on the rear and turret side of this Pz.Kpfw. I Ausf. A identifies the vehicle as belonging to the 1st battalion, 5th Panzer Regiment of the newly formed *5. Leichte Division* (5th Light Division). This is not a command vehicle, but a tank from the so-called *Staffel einer Panzer-Abteilung*, consisting of one Pz.Kpfw. III, one Pz.Kpfw. II and three Pz.Kpfw. I.

Rommel believed that this 'may well have been the theatre in which the war was waged in its most modern guise...It was only in the desert that the principles of armoured warfare as they were taught in theory before the war could be fully applied and thoroughly developed. It was only in the desert that real tank battles were fought by large-scale formations.' Yet while the desert terrain may have suited the unrestricted movement of tracked vehicles, the German tanks rushed to Libya were neither designed for desert operations nor accompanied by sufficient logistical support. The initial 700 kilometre (435 mile) advance caused severe damage to the engines and running gear of the 5th Panzer Regiment tanks with 83 out of 155 tanks disabled, 58 of which required replacement engines. The engine air filters, according to an after-action report, failed to prevent fine sand and dust clogging the crankcases; cylinders and pistons were worn by up to six millimetres. Further problems were caused by sand in the turret races; there were broken shock absorbers and springs, defective fan shaft bearings, and even sixty maintenance requests due to flawed final inspections at factories.

A Pz.Kpfw. III Ausf. G from the 1st Company, 3rd Platoon, 5th Panzer Regiment, is lowered onto the Tripoli dock. Note the original RAL 7021 *Dunkelgrau* (dark grey) paint scheme. RAL was an industrial colour standards scheme introduced in 1927 by the RAL Institute, *Reichs-Ausschuß fur Lieferbedingungen und Gutesicherung*. By the end of the war more than 120 different registrations had been made covering the paints used by the Wehrmacht. A wartime U.S. report erroneously believed that German tanks in North Africa were 'painted black, evidently to aid their antitank gunners in quick daytime identifications while also serving as a night camouflage.'

Note the painted-over former divisional insignia, protective covering over the main gun, and removal of the hull machine gun for the passage across the Mediterranean. The *Fahrgestell* (chassis) number, barely visible on the lower front plate, is 65,214.

Pz.Kpfw. III tactical number '133' – 1st company, 3rd platoon, 3rd vehicle. Note the lighter colour of the hatch interiors. The most common interior colour inside German tanks was *Elfenbein* (ivory) RAL 1001. A former British brigadier believed that the dark external colour was a psychological ruse by Rommel to make the tanks appear more frightening.

The Pz.Kpfw. III Ausf. G (Sd.Kfz. 141) was a 20.3-ton medium tank manufactured from April 1940 to February 1941. Originally designed to mount a 3.7 cm KwK 36 L/46.5 gun, experience gained in Poland and France resulted in the introduction of the heavier 5.0 cm KwK 38 L/42 gun.

The dark grey base colour of these tanks would soon be oversprayed in *Sandgelb* (sand yellow, RAL 8000), and possibly *Graugrün* (grey green, RAL7008), for disruptive camouflage patterns. In the absence of suitable paint, vehicles were sometimes sprayed with oil and then covered with sand. Mud was also used. With regard to camouflage, a post-war retrospective by Wilhelm Willemer advised that 'to camouflage means to disguise for the purpose of deceiving the enemy' with the two-fold aim of preserving combat strength by preventing casualties and increasing the effectiveness of combat strength by adding the factor of surprise. *Tarnung*, the German word for camouflage, means 'not only the disguising of men, equipment and installations, but also the concealment of strategic and tactical intentions'.

A Sd.Kfz. 265 *Kleiner Panzerbefehlswagen* battalion command vehicle from the 1st *Panzerbataillon*. This is the fourth vehicle of the so-called '*Nachrichten-Zug*' (signal communication platoon) of the staff company. It carried a crew of three, including an operator for the FuG6 and FuG2 radio sets, and was armed with a 7.92-mm MG 13 or MG 34 machine gun.

A Pz.Kpfw. II Ausf. C is driven from the wharf under the watchful eye of the *Obergefreiter* closest to the camera. The three-digit identification system identifies this vehicle as belonging to 1st Company, 4th Platoon, 4th vehicle. A post-war report prepared for the U.S. Army observed that the 'black tank uniform was completely unsuitable for camouflage purposes. Its wearer became conspicuous immediately upon leaving his tank.'

An Opel Blitz Type 2.5 – 35 ambulance arrives in Africa. By 1945 German factories had manufactured over 100,000 Blitz trucks in a variety of formats including general-purpose trucks, radio vans, buses and ambulances. Opel – the largest US-owned enterprise in the Third Reich – was the primary supplier of heavy-duty trucks to the Wehrmacht from its Brandenburg factory.

Ammunition and fuel containers in a ship's hold; shortages of both would plague coming Axis operations. Rommel protested outside Tobruk in April that, 'Remarkably, some of my commanders kept wanting to pause so as to take on ammunition, fill up with gasoline and overhaul their vehicles, even when an immediate thrust by us would have had superb chances.' But as Johannes Streich explained: 'There just wasn't any gasoline for Rommel's pipedreams. And that wasn't the fault of "some of" his commanders, but of Rommel himself.' The two German divisions required 24,000 tons of supplies each month; an offensive would require another 20,000 tons; the Luftwaffe needed 9,000 tons and the Italians (civilians and military) 63,000 tons. Tripoli was capable of handling 45,000 tons of stores a month.

The Tripoli waterfront and adjacent railroad terminus. The civilian car parked beside the warehouse is a Lancia Aprilia Berlina.

Ideally, the port of Tripoli would simultaneously handle five cargo ships or four troop ships.

An assortment of Axis transport, including a Fiat 634 civil version (left) and an Opel Blitz 3-tonner 'S'. Near the ship are an Italian Spa TL 37, a light artillery tractor, and a Fiat Type 508 C *Militare* being lowered onto the dock.

Insufficient transport would be a millstone around the neck of the Axis in Rommel's forthcoming operations. Heavy trucks pictured on the left include Fiat Type 634, both civilian and military versions. On the right, five Ford Type 917 Gs are parked in front of older Fords Type V8–51, the first with an open cab.

Italian OM *Autocarretta* Type 36 trucks are pictured on the closest barge; two Lancia 3 RO trucks on the adjacent one.

The OM *Autocarretta* Type 36 was a light military vehicle with four-wheel drive and steering, highly suitable for use in mountainous regions, that was employed as a personnel carrier or gun tractor.

The Sd.Kfz. 231 (8-rad) *schwerer Panzerspähwagen* (heavy reconnaissance armoured car) carried a crew of four and was armed with a 2 cm cannon and MG 34 machine gun. Although suited to desert expanse, it suffered from engine overheating and high fuel consumption, which limited its radius of action. Note the *Pakschutz*: an 8-mm V-shaped armoured shield intended to provide additional frontal protection against anti-tank shells.

Show of force. A Sd. Kfz. 7 half-track towing an 8.8 cm Flak before the assembled Tripoli crowd. The Phoenicians founded the Libyan capital around 500 BC. Centuries later in October 1911, Italian marines invaded Ottoman-held Tripoli, an affront to a young, disapproving Benito Mussolini. 'Every honest Socialist must disapprove of this Libyan adventure. It means only useless and stupid bloodshed', he ironically avowed.

A parade before Rommel and Italo Gariboldi, Governor General of Libya, of newly arrived Axis vehicles. The Italian car in the foreground is a Fiat 1500.

Chapter Two
An Unfamiliar Battlefield

Prior to the outbreak of hostilities in 1939, Germany had undertaken virtually no preparation for the conduct of land warfare outside Europe. According to former intelligence officer Hans-Otto Behrendt, 'rarely has one general known as little about an enemy and his territory as Rommel did' when he first arrived on African soil. Rommel, as a consequence, was frequently airborne over the battlefield in a Fieseler Fi 156 *Storch* (stork), one of the most recognisable German aircraft of the war. A lightweight plane that excelled in liaison, reconnaissance, communications, ambulance and personal transport roles, it was renowned for its remarkable short takeoff and landing (STOL) performance on rough, ad hoc landing strips inaccessible to other aircraft. The Fi 156's best defense against enemy aircraft was its manoeuvrability and ability to slow to around 60 kph, a speed at which enemy fighters would stall. A *Storch* featured in the daring rescue of Benito Mussolini, imprisoned at Gran Sasso d'Italia in the Abruzzi Apennines, in September 1943.

Rear view of a Fi 156 C-2 with *Verbandskennzeichen* (operational code) 5F + YK apparently altered to 5F + XK and belonging to 2.(H)/*Aufklärungsgruppe* 14, 'H' referring to *Heeres*, or Army. This model was adapted for tropical use by the addition of filtered air intakes. Note the 7.92mm MG 15 machine gun mounted in the rear of cabin.

A smiling *Oberst* Claus von dem Borne, Chief of Staff of the Afrikakorps from 1 March 1941 to 5 October 1941, poses before 5F + XK. Other German reconnaissance aircraft used in North Africa included the Henschel Hs 126 and the Focke-Wulf Fw 189.

The high wing and angular windows of the extensively glazed Fi 156 cabin afforded the pilot and two passengers an excellent field of vision. *Leutnant* Hermann Aldinger recounted an incident when Rommel signalled a pilot to 'go lower'. Italian troops below, in error, began firing at the aircraft: 'Bullets began hitting the wings, and with a burst of aerobatics the pilot just managed to get the hell out of it.'

Aerial view of an armoured column snaking its way along the Via Balbia. This strategic coastal road ran between the Tunisian and Egyptian frontiers of Mussolini's Libyan colony. Riddled with potholes, it was often impassable after heavy rains and frequently overflown by enemy aircraft.

Miles of featureless desert; a vast and unfamiliar battlefield that thrust Rommel and the *Afrikakorps*, one of the most romanticised German formations of the war, to prominence.

Two images taken from an Italian Caproni Ca.309 *Ghibli* ('Desert Wind') above the *Arco dei Fileni*, Italo Balbo's monumental arch delineating the Cyrenaica and Tripolitania frontiers. Unveiled before il Duce on 16 March 1937, the relic from Italian colonialism was demolished by Muammar Gaddafi in 1973.

Fi 156 bearing *Verbandskennzeichen* 5F+UK was another aircraft operated by
2.(H)/*Aufklärungsgruppe* 14. Friedrich von Mellenthin recalled one occasion when Rommel flew
over a formation that had stopped for no apparent reason. A signed message dropped from his
Storch warned 'unless you get going at once I shall come down'.

Italian aircraft on the ground, possibly in Tripoli, include two three-engined Savoia-Marchetti S.73s (one destroyed) and one of only three four-engined S.74s produced as a civilian transport pressed into service by the *Regia Aeronautica*.

Motorcyclists, wild camels and razorback dunes. Wrote Schraepler: '[*Leutnant* Hermann Aldinger] and Rommel were flying in thickest fog yesterday. They had the impression they came within a hair's breadth of death. It was gusty, so they had to fly very low. They survived by succeeding in passing the crest of the dunes and mountains.'

Taking off beside an encamped headquarters position. Note the *Mammut* (Mammoth), Pz.Kpfw. III, and the degree of spacing between the tents and vehicles in case of aerial attack.

A pause in the fighting. Rommel had urged his Panzers forward before the fighting at Mechili in April 1941, having determined that the 'desert tracks are passable. I have flown over them myself.'

'The generation of dust', reported Toppe, 'made it practically impossible to conceal marching columns. Dust clouds could be seen even at great distances and enabled one to recognize the size of the columns and sometimes even the type of vehicles (wheeled or tracklaying).'

Soldiers wave from a newly constructed fixed defensive position. This was a typical reinforced squad strongpoint, constructed for all-round defence and measuring roughly forty-five to sixty-five metres across. An anti-tank gun would be sited in the central position.

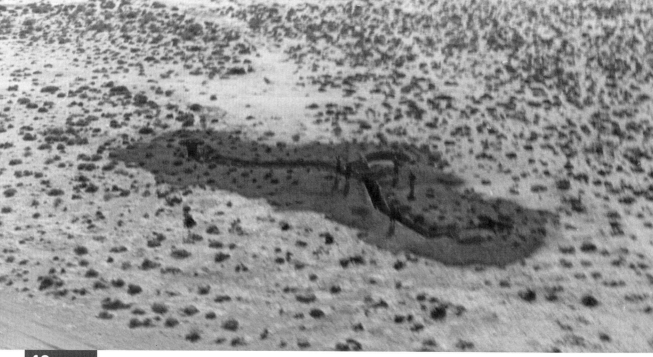

Chapter Three
The 'Desert Fox'

Erwin Rommel was appointed commander-in-chief of the *Afrikakorps* on 3 February 1941. Nine days later he flew into Tripoli's Castel Benito airport. Newly arrived, we find the future 'Desert Fox' (centre) still wearing his continental-style uniform, soon to be replaced by a tailored tropical version. Pictured on Rommel's right (above) is *Oberst* Rudolf Schmundt (Hitler's adjutant and a casualty of the 20 July 1944 bomb plot)—the first two German officers to arrive on African soil. Schmundt's presence increased Rommel's authority with both senior Italian and German officers.

Tripoli. 'Only high-grade officers were posted to Africa,' Siegfried Westphal recalled, 'so that the personality and ability of all the remaining generals of the Africa Army were above the average. Altogether, eight generals were killed in Africa, a high figure when one considers the comparatively small total of casualties.'

In the words of an Italian army doctor: 'We had been awaiting the British fatalistically – almost gladly. At least the whole business would be over. But the Germans came instead.'

Major Hans-Joachim Schraepler observed on 21 February 1941 that Rommel (centre) 'is an impressive and also an impressing personality. If only our troops would arrive here soon. The current difficulties of competence with the Italian troops were removed. They will, of course, never stop. Rommel has great plans.' Rommel is pictured between *Oberst* Claus von dem Borne and *Generale d'Armata* Italo Gariboldi, Governor General of Libya.

Hans Freiherr von Eseback penned a description of Rommel: 'He has a high, symmetrical forehead, a forceful nose, prominent cheekbones, a narrow mouth with tight lips and a chin that juts defiance. There are hard lines from his nostrils to the corners of his mouth, but they are softened by something often akin to an artful smile. And in his clear blue eyes too, cold and appraising, penetrating and keen, there is something of a cunning that brings real warmth to this man's features when it breaks through.'

Pictured on Rommel's left is General Johannes Streich, commander of the 5th Light Division, with his *Ritterkreuz* prominently displayed.

Contradicting British expectations and his own Axis directives, on 30 March 1941 Rommel ordered Streich to march on Marsa Brega. A tempestuous relationship between the two men ensued. A week later Streich refused to attack the former Turkish fort at Mechili on the basis that many of his division's vehicles had broken down during the march from Tripoli. An infuriated Rommel responded with accusations of cowardice; Streich responded by removing his Knight's Cross and shouting, 'Withdraw that remark or I'll throw this at your feet.' A half-hearted apology followed. Rommel later relieved Streich of his command in mid-May (after failing to take Tobruk) because he was 'too concerned' over his men's welfare, an accusation to which the latter is said to have snapped, 'I can imagine no greater words of praise for a division commander.' Rommel's own aide later wrote that he liked the 'friendly and considerate Streich', whom he regarded as 'extremely brave', though ill-treated 'so remorselessly'. In fairness to Rommel's rebuke, it should be remembered that Streich was later censured by General Heinz Guderian for his unhurried advance on Germany's Eastern Front.

Rommel received the Italian Silver Medal of Military Valor from General Attilio Teruzzi, Minister for Italian Africa 1939–43, on 22 April 1941. Unimpressed, he groaned in a letter to his wife, Lu, that it was a trivial business at a 'time like this' during the heavy fighting at Tobruk. Earlier in the same letter he poured scorn on his Axis ally: 'There's little reliance to be placed on the Italian troops. They're extremely sensitive to enemy tanks and – as in 1917 – quick to throw up the sponge.' Yet he had flung the Italians against Tobruk's outer defences after his own men had failed – but they too made no impression. In situations where the Germans had failed, the Italians became convenient scapegoats. He even issued an order 'much discussed and disputed in high Italian circles' that in the future he would 'expect the immediate execution of officers who showed cowardice in the face of the enemy.'

Newly decorated—another photo opportunity to present an outward picture of Axis solidarity. Rommel is flanked by Generals Mario Roatta (left) and Attilio Teruzzi.

From the outset, 49-year-old Rommel was at odds with Gariboldi (centre) his nominal superior. (Gariboldi's predecessor, Marshal Rodolfo Graziani, resigned after the annihilation of his Tenth Army by the British). Whereas Gariboldi advocated a defensive cordon around Tripoli, Rommel looked hungrily to the east – the lure of the Nile.

15 May 1941. Rommel travelled to Cyrene for a meeting with Gariboldi in his hotel. In the presence of the officer corps in the hotel lobby, the Italian commander was awarded the Iron Cross First and Second Class. 'He was pleased and visibly moved,' Schraepler recorded. A fine lunch was followed by cheese, coffee and wines, the Italians 'not aware of the war' the German officer mocked. Three days earlier Gariboldi had decorated Rommel with Italy's highest Gallantry award – the Military Order of Savoy, Grand Officer – in a large outdoor ceremony recorded by newsreel cameramen. Twenty-seven months later Italy signed an unconditional armistice with the Allies; a Free French newspaper sarcastically paraphrased Machiavelli: 'The House of Savoy never finished a war on the same side it started, unless the war lasted long enough to change sides twice.'

Tourists in uniform. Rommel is shown around the ancient ruins of Cyrene, including the Temple of Zeus, by his newly decorated host, Italo Gariboldi. The German officer (far right) is *Oberst* Heinz Heggenreiner.

Behind the scenes, Rommel was 'berated violently' by Gariboldi for disobeying orders from Rome, and for failing to take into account the vulnerable supply situation. But as Rommel later wrote, he had no intention of 'allowing good opportunities to slip by unused'.

Gariboldi (on Rommel's right) was relieved on 19 July 1941 because of his purported lack of cooperation with Rommel. Replaced by Ettore Bastico, Gariboldi was transferred to the Soviet Union where he assumed command of the *Armata Italiana in Russia* or ARMIR.

The British anti-gas goggles adorning Rommel's peak cap were rather flimsy, suggesting that he in fact owned several different pairs.

Rommel pictured decorating four Italian officers with the Iron Cross Second Class. Note that he wears the Italian *sahariana* jacket and grey-green *Schirmmütze* (peaked cap). The vehicle visible in the rear is an Italian Ceirano CM 50 workshop truck.

Three awarded Italian officers and one colonial officer photographed post ceremony. Interestingly, Rommel's adjutant complained in a letter home on 2 June 1941 of the contested decision by Berlin to stop further decorations for the *Afrikakorps* – 'conducting a war of leisure' – on the grounds that sufficient had already been received.

Rommel addresses General Gastone Gambara (centre) and Marshal Ettore Bastico, recipients of the Iron Cross First and Second Class. Gambara, a veteran of the First World War and Spanish Civil War, became Chief of General Staff in Libya to Bastico in October 1941. As Albert Kesselring observed, discord between General Rommel and Marshal Bastico 'aggravated matters'. Bastico was demoted from commander-in-chief North Africa to Governor General of Libya in February 1942.

The Italian commanders-in-chief. According to Westphal, 'first Gariboldi and later Marshal Bastico, did their best to give a wide freedom of action to Rommel as the commander at the front. Sometimes they went almost too far in doing so. For instance, in 1941 it was not Bastico who wanted to reach the Nile. Like his predecessor, Bastico saw as his task to give as much assistance to the German command at the front as his resources allowed.'

Rommel, seen congratulating Marshal Ettore Bastico, received his third Italian decoration from Bastico; 'He awarded me the Colonial Order by command of the king. A big silver star, bigger than the last one, and a red sash with small emblems. I've really got enough of that stuff now.'

Oberst Heinz Heggenreiner (in the centre between Gariboldi and Rommel), former German Military Attaché in Rome, was Rommel's liaison officer with the Italian command.

A newsreel camera crew follow Rommel during an award ceremony. German officers were frequently critical of their Axis counterparts. Wrote Siegfried Westphal: 'They lived in a world of their own, having only the slightest contact with their men. In general, the more senior officers were well-trained and level-headed, but they lacked the tools of their trade. The abilities of the junior officers were less satisfactory'; they had 'no close contact with their men'. Hans-Joachim Schraepler believed if they were 'more courageous, their troops would be pretty good. They are always delighted when they see German officers welcoming us with 'camerada'. Their soldiers, extremely helpful, love to be commanded. If there is no leadership and no model, the result cannot be good. For us, this is not enough. We require proper training, education and a sense of duty.' There was also a deep cultural divide between the two armies. While the Italians have a 'cheerful, amiable disposition', Hans von Luck noted, 'they are of a different mentality from us Germans.'

Generalmajor Heinrich Kirchheim, saluting, fell foul of Rommel after the abortive mid-May 1941 assault on Tobruk. In a letter to General Franz Halder, Chief of the General Staff, Kirchheim complained that 'Rommel is in no way up to his command duties. All day long he races about between his widely scattered forces, ordering raids and dissipating his troops. No one at all has a a general overview of the distribution of his forces and of their fighting strength…partial advances by weak Panzer forces have resulted in substanial losses…' Kirchheim's replacement was *Generalmajor* Johann von Ravenstein, a First World War veteran awarded the Knight's Cross during the Battle of France.

Informal portraits of Rommel and his Italian allies .
German-born writer Rosie Goldschmidt Waldeck wrote
in 1943 of the former's 'indelible youthfulness'.

Rommel was a veritable gift to Nazi propaganda. Here was a charismatic tank commander tackling the stubborn British foe in an exotic theatre of war that fascinated the German public.

Pictured with his back to a *Mammut,* also wearing the Knight's Cross and *Pour le Mérite*, is Generalmajor Johann von Ravenstein, commander of the 5th Light Division. This particular formation was reorganised and reinforced as the 21st Panzer Division on 1 October 1941. Ravenstein was subsequently captured by New Zealand troops on 29 November 1941 on his way to a staff conference near Tobruk. Rommel's officers paid a heavy price for 'leading from the front'—between 18 November 1941 and 20 February 1942 the 21st Panzer Division lost 47 officers killed, 61 wounded and 40 missing.

Seated opposite Rommel is *Generalmajor* Philipp Müller-Gebhard, deputy leader of *Panzergruppe Afrika*, in place of *Generalmajor* Walter Neumann-Silkow, who was on sick leave for three weeks.

Generalmajor Johann von Ravenstein, commander of the 21st Panzer Division, photographed at Tobruk shortly after his capture by New Zealand troops. Never a fan of Rommel, he spoke of the 'great losses in recent fighting, mismanagement and disorganization, and above all, dissatisfaction with Rommel's leadership.' Ravenstein spent the remainder of the war in a Canadian prisoner of war camp.

Senior DAK officers. Left to right: Siegfried Westphal, Friedrich-Wilhelm von Mellenthin, and Ludwig Crüwell. In his 1950 book, *Heer in Fesseln,* Westphal reflected upon his time in North Africa. With regard to the secret of Rommel's 'magnetism', the answer, he believed, was simple: it lay in his 'personality and actions. For this man was indeed a personality, who could have been exactly suited for this task in Africa even without desert experience – and of this he gained enough and to spare. It was his strong will, relentless even towards himself, which, despite all difficulties, made the Army capable of achievements whose magnitude even the enemy acknowledged. No one but Rommel could have made such demands on the soldiers. They followed him because they knew he did not spare himself, because they saw him daily in their midst, and because he was a born leader…naturally he was not free from faults. Everyone knows that where there is much light there must be shadows. For instance, in his success he often aimed too high, forgetting the limits which are imposed by such factors as supply. Moreover he was frequently unjust if a measure which he had ordered failed to achieve the success which he had promised himself from it. In such cases he was prone to seek the cause not in the material difficulties but in the faulty execution…Nor was Rommel free from personal ambition and a certain vanity. His strongly-developed spirit of contrariness and his occasional pig-headedness often made it difficult for both superiors and subordinates to get along with him. And, finally, he was no diplomat. He said what he thought bluntly, and in the heat of the moment he must have frequently offended our allies when he had something to complain about.'

Encamped near Tobruk. The Italian equipment, Hans-Joachim Schraepler noted on 30 March 1941, 'with tents, field chairs and a kitchen, is so incomparably more luxurious than ours. In their tents one can move, they are comfortable, with folding wash-stands and much more. The Italians have, of course, long experience in the desert. They know what one needs.'

Rommel, pictured by the Mediterraean, led a spartan existence. Usually dining by himself or in the company of his closest staff officers, Rommel 'indulged' in having a single glass of wine, his diet, otherwise, the same as that of the ordinary soldier. A demading leader, in July 1941, having failed to storm Tobruk, he charged, 'During the offensive in Cyrenaica and particularly during the early part of the siege of Tobruk, there were numerous instances when my clear and specific orders were not obeyed by my commanders, or not promptly; there were instances bordering on disobedience, and some commanders broke down in the face of the enemy.'

Surveying the battlefield. Schmidt: 'The General inspired all ranks with enthusiasm and energy wherever he appeared. He could not tolerate subordinates who were not as enthusiatic and active as himself, and he was merciless in his treatment of anybody who displayed lack of initiative. Out! Back to Germany they went at once.'

Striking a familiar pose for the camera, Rommel directs his Italian entourage. Although taken by a German *Propaganda-Kompanie* (PK) photographer, the image ran counter to directives given to PK photographers on the Eastern Front who, for example, photographed advancing columns moving from left to right to mirror Hitler's eastward drive across the USSR.

Rommel's 'strange ideas on the priciples of staff work', noted Mellenthin, included his 'particularly irksome characteristic' of interfering in details that should 'have been the responsibilty of the chief of staff. As a rule Rommel expected his chief of staff to accompany him on his visits to the front— which frequently meant into the very forefront of the battle. This was contrary to the accepted general staff principle, that the chief of staff is the deputy of the commander-in-chief during the latter's absence. But Rommel liked to have his principal adviser always at his elbow, and if he became a casuality, well—he could always be replaced.'

A difficult alliance. Rommel's series of rapid promotions in North Africa touched a raw nerve with Mussolini's generals. Rommel himself had little respect for the Italians, perhaps as a consequence of his First World War experience. 'Many Italian officers had thought of war as little more than a pleasant adventure,' he wrote, 'and were, perforce, having to suffer a bitter disillusionment.' Noted Goebbels: 'Rommel gives the most denigrating judgement of the Italians. He thinks nothing of them.'

Rommel greets Colonel Ugo Montemurro, commander of the 8th Bersaglieri Regiment. Rommel recorded: 'Here in North Africa, the Italian Bersaglieri has aroused the German soldier's admiration.' The M1935 colonial helmet (*casco coloniale*) is adorned with cockerel feathers (*plumetti*).

Poring over maps before assembled Italian officers including Attilio Teruzzi and Gariboldi.

Rommel was a 'master of deception and disguises', *Leutnant* Alfred Berndt lauded in a propaganda broadcast. 'If the enemy believe we are particularly strong at one place, then you can be sure we are weak. If they think we are weak, and venture close to us, then we are definitely strong. "With your general we just didn't know where we were!", that's what one British prisoner complained.'

Inspecting a 10 cm *Kanone* 18 battery. Rommel, Mellenthin observed, noted 'everything' during his visits to the front; 'nothing escaped him…When a gun was inadequately camoflaged, when mines were laid in insufficient number, or when a standing patrol did not have ammunition, Rommel would see to it. Everywhere he convinced himself personally that his orders were being carried out. While very popular with young soldiers and NCOs with whom he cracked many a joke, he could become most outspoken and very offensive to commanders of troops if he did not approve of their measures.'

'Boiling with impatience', Rommel's vitality impressed many of his subordinate officers. Mellenthin recorded that his energy was 'something to marvel at; he usually spent the whole day on such inspections – regardless of the scorching heat which during the summer months sometimes reached 110 degrees [Fahrenheit or 43°C] in the shade.' Like many of his fellow *Afrikaner*, however, Rommel soon succumbed to the ravages of jaundice, while Berlin, ignorant of the harsh desert conditions, complained of the high turnover of DAK soldiers.

Inspecting fortifications at Bardia. The former Italian fortress, captured in January by the British, was occupied by Axis forces on 14 April 1941.

For many, the desert cold came as a shock. Hans von Luck remembered how he 'got used to the cold nights. We didn't take off our tropical [great]coats, and thick non-regulation scarves, until well into the morning when the heat had slowly worked through them. This was the thermos principle, which we had learned observing the Bedouins'.

Silhouetted against the sky, Rommel and his staff are pictured in two models of the *mittlerer geländegängiger Personenkraftwagen* (medium cross-country passenger car): on the left, an Auto Union/Horch 901 Type 40, with a single spare wheel stowed inside the car body; on the right, an early production model 901 with the distinctive outer spare wheel.

Rommel (pictured above in an early production model Auto Union/Horch Type 901) escaped numerous brushes with death, unscathed while those nearby fell. His adjutant penned a letter on 22 April 1941 that he had buried 'two drivers at a nice spot on the big road [the Via Balbia] at kilometre stone 31.'

Rommel characteristically led his units from the front, racing between individual command posts. *Oberleutnant* Harald Kuhn (5th Panzer Regiment) recalled in his memoirs how Rommel could be 'found in even the most dangerous situations – it was said that he had five drivers shot out next to him in his vehicle.'

An iconic PK photograph of the 'Desert Fox'. Wearing a bleached cap (right) was Rommel's longterm driver, *Unteroffizier* Hellmut von Leipzig. Born in Namibia, Leipzig volunteered to join the *Afrikakorps*. 'I wanted to return to Africa,' he explained in a 2001 interview at his African home. Arriving in North Africa in October 1941, Leipzig was ordered to undertake a test drive with Rommel, an incident in which both front tyres were shot through, but which secured him the role. If possible, Rommel 'wrote a letter to his wife every day while being driven,' Leipzig recalled. On another occasion, driving through an artillery barrage, Rommel suddenly fell backwards. A shell splinter struck his binoculars and leather coat before hitting his abdomen. 'When he recovered a medic placed a plaster on the wound…he was not reckless but often put his life at risk.' Although Leipzig was impressed by Rommel's Spartan character, he was often shocked by his harshness towards his senior officers; 'Rommel was not an easy boss'. One of his 'ablest officers' who requested four days leave after his family was killed in a bombing raid on Düsseldorf was told: 'My dear Colonel, at home you can not do anything anymore, but here I need you on the advance when the lives of thousands of men are at stake.' Similarly, Leipzig was astonished when he introduced him to his older brother Konrad, an amputee. Rommel purportedly told Leipzig that his brother should quickly leave North Africa, lest the British believe that the DAK was fielding cripples at the front! Leipzig ferried Rommel to an airfield near Tunis in March 1943 as he departed North Africa. His last words to his driver: 'You will go to Germany to the military academy, I have arranged everything.'

Leipzig subsequently fought in Europe as a *Leutnant* in the Division Brandenburg. Awarded the Knight's Cross on 28 April 1945, he was captured by Red Army troops and finally released from captivity in 1955. In 2001, the then 84-year-old fondly reminisced how the Horch was an extremely robust vehicle, with folding rear seats.

There existed a 'mutual understanding' between Rommel (seen here in his Sd.Kfz. 250/3) and frontline troops, recalled Mellenthin, which 'cannot be explained and analysed, but which is a gift of the gods. The *Afrikakorps* followed him wherever he led, however hard he drove them…the men knew that Rommel was the last man Rommel spared; they saw him in their midst and they felt, "This is our leader".'

The bleached caps and tanned skin of veteran *Afrikaner*. Rumours abounded at the time in Allied circles that Rommel was leading a corps d'élite of specially trained German desert warriors. The DAK, however, was formed 'without experience' or formal training during the spring of 1941. Berlin had accumulated only scant information on Libya, as the area fell within the Italian sphere of interest. The formations dispatched to Libya were those available for immediate deployment.

Hermann Aldinger recorded the appreciation felt by Rommel's visits to the front lines: 'The troops stand to attention and salute, and are delighted when the general speaks to them…the general feels the urge to meet the men actually face-to-face with the enemy, he has to speak with them…You can see the real pleasure on their faces, when these ordinary soldiers are allowed to speak in person to their general…' In a similar vein, von Esebeck recalled in 1944 that 'there is a strange magic strength that this soldier radiates to his troops right down to the last rifleman.'

An image taken from the German propaganda magazine *Signal* shows Rommel jumping from a knocked-out British Cruiser tank. Note the Tropenhelm (tropical helmet) in place of his usual peaked cap, an unpopular piece of headgear usually discarded by German troops at the front.

Rommel enjoyed the attention of the press. No other German general featured so heavily, or willingly, in photographs taken in the field. Familiar themes included troop inspections, the viewing of captured materiel, or shots of the general poring over maps or gesticulating towards the distant horizon. Rommel was acutely aware of the power of propaganda in developing his career and reputation. He assiduously courted the Nazi media machine, Joseph Goebbels' the *Reichsministerium für Volksaufklärung und Propaganda*, acutely aware that his position in the German army was entirely dependent on Hitler's patronage. He also earned the admiration of Winston Churchill, who in a speech to the House of Commons in January 1942 expressed that 'we have a very daring and skillful opponent against us, and may I say across the havoc of war, a great general.'

Frustration over Rommel's leadership style surfaced long before the desert legend did. Unlike the charismatic image so often projected in books and on film, Rommel was a demanding, often maddening commander to work under. Somewhat of a loose cannon in General Fritz Halder's eyes, Rommel was a general who needed reining in. Halder's growing frustration reads in a diary entry of 23 April: 'Rommel has not sent in a single clear report, and I have a feeling that things are in a mess... All day long he rushes about between his widely scattered units and stages reconnaissance raids in which he fritters away his strength... the piecemeal thrusts of weak armoured forces have been costly... His motor vehicles are in poor condition and many of the tank engines need replacing... It is essential to have the situation cleared up without delay.' To investigate this 'mess', Halder dispatched *Generalleutnant* Friedrich Paulus, who was on good terms with Rommel, and, as Halder thought, 'perhaps the only man with enough personal influence to head off this soldier gone stark mad...'

Field Marshal Walter von Brauchitsch, commander-in-chief of the German Army, was similarly unimpressed with Rommel's leadership. Quick to apportion blame on subordinate officers who failed to meet his demanding, sometimes unrealistic expectations, Rommel sent many home packing. A reprimanding communique detailed his '...court martial decisions and complaints, and especially... the numerous requests to relieve officers of high assessement and proven reliability, even taking into consideration the special... roughness required in leadership in these cases... The more difficult the conditions are, the more nerves are stretched. It is all the more the duty of every superior to check closely whether interventions such as threats or requests to relieve battle-proven officers or harsh criticism or hasty orders are appropriate; whether an instructive conversation carried on in a fraternal spirit without any edge to it would be more likely to accomplish the aim. I consider it my duty not only in the interests of the *Afrikakorps* but also in your personal interest to bring these points to your attention.' Unimpressed, Brauchitsch questioned whether Rommel's leadership squabbles were a consequence of the extreme heat.

General Bodewin Keitel, head of the Wehrmacht's personnel department, circulated a memorandum regarding Rommel's strategic myopia and hasty removal of senior officers: 'For all [his] exceptional personal courage and willingness to take tough decisions, it seems to me that he lacks the broad view. Because of this he gives orders that have to be rescinded shortly afterwards, because they were ill-considered and impossible to carry out. The second and even more serious point is the coarse and abrasive manner in which he insults the honour of older and trusted commanders. He is given to making judgements such as; " I am obliged to remove you from your command", or he makes hasty decisions to dismiss officers and not infrequently calls for a court martial for cowardice.'

Generalmajor Walter Neumann-Silkow (left) assumed command of the 15th Panzer Division from *Oberst* Maximilian von Herff on 16 June 1941. A popular and highly decorated leader, Neumann-Silkow was mortally wounded by British artillery fire during the final days of the 1941 siege of Tobruk. He died on 9 December 1941, the second original DAK divisional commander to fall, and was posthumously promoted to *Generalleutnant*. Herff subsequently condemned Rommel's 'grotesque decisions', 'erratic leadership' and the court-martialling of senior commanders who failed to meet Rommel's standards. 'We are all horrified about it,' he declared; 'A lot of the more impulsive commands issued by *Afrikakorps* we junior officers just don't make head or tail of.'

Rommel is seated between a pensive *Generalmajor* Alfred Gause (left) and *Generalmajor* Walter Neumann-Silkow. Post-war, Gause credited Rommel's method of command to his 'almost one-sidedly developed military frame of mind and a certain measure of audacity, combined with ability and flexibility in the exploitation of favourable situations and an extraordinarily instinctive sense for terrain and the enemy situation.'

Gause and Rommel pictured amid a battlefield strewn with wrecked Axis and Allied vehicles. Although Rommel took care not to become too close with his subordinates, a bond developed between the pair. Rommel even wrote to Gause while he was convalescing in Europe from wounds suffered during the battles around the British Gazala line. Upon his return to Africa, Gause became chief of staff of *Heeresgruppe Afrika* (Army Group Africa) on 1 March 1943. When recalled to Europe, Rommel selected Gause as his chief of staff. In November 1944 he was relieved of his duties, apparently because of his loyalty to Rommel amid the 20 July conspiracy to kill Hitler. In the closing months of the war he attended a corps commanders' training course before his final (hopeless) assignment of leading an isolated German corps trapped far behind the Russian lines.

Situational briefing. Hans von Luck recalled the strain of battle of Gause (pictured on Rommel's right); he 'looked tired and emaciated. It had been particularly hard for him to make the right decisions when Rommel was "leading from the front" and out of reach, often for days on end.'

Rommel and Gause share a coffee. Note the captured *Mammut* in the background.

Facing Rommel is *Generalmajor* Max Sümmermann, commander of the 90th Light 'Afrika' Division. Sümmermann was killed in a rearguard air raid on 10 December 1941 during the retreat from Cyrenaica, his last words purportedly: 'I have a son in Russia.' Sümmermann was replaced by *Generalleutnant* Richard Veith, who in turn was relieved of his command on 10 April 1942.

Closest to the camera is Major Friedrich von Mellenthin, a member of the *Panzergruppe* staff who arrived in Africa in June 1941 to serve in Rommel's headquarters. Mellenthin later recalled how Rommel 'was not an easy man to serve; he spared those around him as little as he spared himself. An iron constitution and nerves of steel were needed...' He also commented that he was never as nice or polite as the charactaer James Mason portrayed in the 1951 movie *The Desert Fox: The Story of Rommel*.

Wearing the *Tropenhelm* is Rommel's interpreter, *Sonderführer* Dr. Ernst Franz.

Western Desert deliberation. Schraepler recorded the rocky relationship (on 29 April 1941) behind the cordial façade painted by propaganda photographs: 'Cooperation with our Italian allies is too difficult. Everything has to be considered down to the smallest detail and to be harmonised.' Note the Opel Admiral cabriolet in the rear displaying a corps commander's flag and general's pennant.

Staff conferences. Mellenthin (above, wearing circular goggles) wrote after the war that Rommel was the 'ideal commander for desert warfare. His custom of "leading from the front" occasionally told against him; decisions affecting the army as a whole were sometimes influenced unduly by purely local successes or failures. On the other hand, by going himself to the danger spot—and he had an uncanny faculty for appearing at the right place at the right time—he was able to adapt his plans to new situations, and in the fluid conditions of the Western Desert this was a factor of supreme importance.'

Rommel in conversation with *Oberstleutnant* Otto Heymer. Heymer, Rommel's *Koluft*, or Luftwaffe advisor, was awarded the Knight's Cross on 13 April 1941.

Luftwaffe *Generalmajor* Stefan Fröhlich (in *Fliegermütze*, the Luftwaffe side cap) was *Fliegerführer Afrika* from 24 April 1941 to 10 April 1942.

Interservice meeting in Derna, 30 September 1941. From left to right: Stefan Fröhlich, *General der Flieger* Hans Geisler (commander of X *Fliegerkorps* from 2 October 1939 to 31 August 1942), Rommel, Siegfried Westphal (partially hidden) and Alfred Gause. Of the five men, all survived the war with the exception of Rommel.

Rommel's command methods often left Siegfried Westphal (far left) with responsibilities beyond his rank and position. On 25 November 1941, for example, unable to contact Rommel, Gause or General Ludwig Crüwell, Westphal reversed Rommel's standing orders – at considerable risk to his career – and directed Ravenstein's 21st Panzer Division to return to the Tobruk sector. Rommel was furious when he learned of his unauthorised intervention, though he later relented, even acknowledging that Westphal's decision was correct.

Bespectacled Italian officer, General Carlo Calvi di Bergolo, son-in-law of the Italian King, commanded the 131st 'Centauro' Armoured Division in 1942. Switching sides after the Italian armistice, Calvi di Bergolo surrendered the Open City of Rome to Albert Kesselring on 10 September 1943.

With Rommel in the desert, to his right Siegfried Westphal and Alfred Gause.

Rommel requested that Fritz Bayerlein (far right), a veteran of campaigns in Poland, France and Russia, serve as chief of staff to the commander of the *Afrikakorps*. After the Axis capitulation in Tunisia in May 1943, Bayerlein fought on the Eastern Front, Normandy and in the Ardennes offensive. He surrendered to U.S. forces in April 1945. To his right is Generalmajor Walter Neumann-Silkow. Standing with his back to the camera is Ludwig Crüwell.

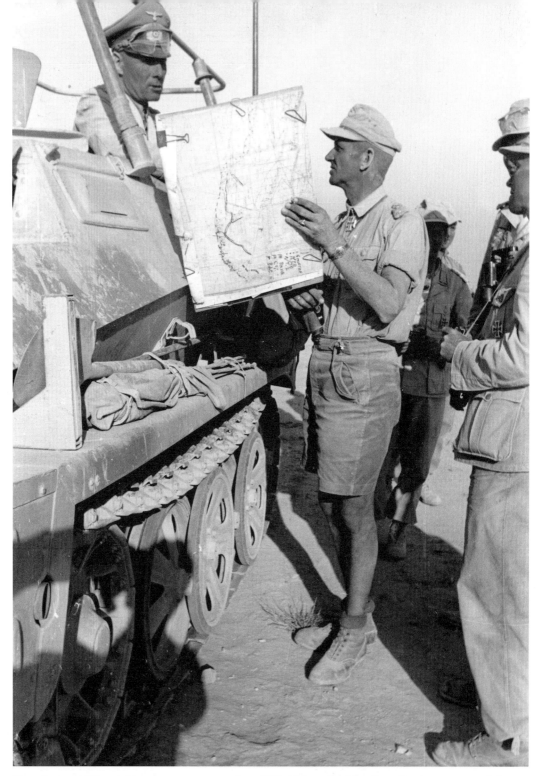

Oberstleutnant Eduard Crasemann, commander of 33rd Motorised Artillery Regiment, part of the 15th Panzer Division, discusses a situation map with Rommel. Crasemann was awarded the Knight's Cross on 26 December 1941. For a period in July–August, Crasemann was given command of the 15th Panzer Division before combat wounds forced his return to Germany. Captured in the Ruhr pocket in April 1945, he was later convicted of the execution of 162 Italians in 1944 and sentenced to 10 years' imprisonment. Crasemann died in Werl Prison on 28 April 1950.

Bespectacled *Generalmajor* Karl Böttcher was appointed commander of the 104th Artillery Command on 30 September 1939. Despite his inexperience commanding armour, Rommel placed Böttcher in temporary command of the 21st Panzer Division on 1 December 1941 following Ravenstein's capture. Böttcher was awarded the Knight's Cross on 13 December 1941. (Rommel's adjutant reflected on the task of preparing a proposal for such an award – producing a convincing case in combination with an understanding of strategy and a thorough grasp of the circumstances in which the medal was earned). Böttcher ended the war as commanding general of the 4th Special Purposes Artillery Command before surrendering to British forces on 8 May 1945.

Major Hans von Luck und Witten arrived in Africa on 8 April 1942 to assume command of the 3rd Panzer Reconnaissance Battalion and was injured in the groin by a shell splinter on 27 May 1942. Continuing to command with the help of morphine injections, his wound became infected. 'While two sisters held me tight, the doctor, who seemed to me like a butcher, began to cut away at my wound. I cried out like an animal and thought I would faint with pain.' Invalided home on a hospital ship, Luck returned to Africa in mid-September 1942 where he once again led the 3rd Panzer Reconnaissance Battalion. Following Rommel's defeat in the Second Battle of Alamein, Luck helped to screen the Axis withdrawal back to Tripoli and beyond into Tunisia. In March 1943 he travelled to Germany to unsuccessfully appeal to Hitler about an evacuation plan worked out by Rommel and *Generaloberst* Hans-Jurgen von Armin, a German 'Dunkirk'. Refused a meeting with the Führer, Luck stayed in Europe, later commanding the 21st Panzer Division. Surrendering to Soviet forces on 27 April 1945, he was discharged in January 1950.

Rommel and his staff officers, including Majors Hans-Joachim Schraepler and Wustefeld, outside the Bardia mosque. Note the lighter coloured Italian *Sahariana* jacket (centre).

Rommel pictured with map board under his arm. The maps intially supplied by the Italians were of dubious accuracy.

Hans von Luck recalled collecting his tropical uniform: 'What we were "fitted" out with defies description. One could see that Germany had no longer any colonies since 1918, and so had no idea of what was suitable for the tropics. We need only to have asked our allies, the Italians, but no, the commissariat had designed the tropical equipment strictly in the Prussian mode: khaki-coloured, tight-fitting uniform of close material with a linen belt and high lace-up boots. In addition, a pith helmet, which, according to long standing opinion, was essential wear in the tropics. Along with the other pieces, shirts impermeable to air, a brown tie, etc., we acknowledged receipt of our equipment and returned to the barracks to stage a fashion show. Wounded men from North Africa, waiting there for reposting, told us how they, like many others, had carried on a lively trade with the Italians in order to exchange at least some of their equipment for the more appropriate Italian uniforms…'

Generalmajor Fritz Bayerlein (centre). Much to the frustration of his staff, Rommel would on occasion leave his headquarters and disappear into the desert for several days, leading like the 'head of a commando' rather than a commanding officer. Bayerlein recalled a lengthy search for Rommel that eventually found him and his chief of staff in a British truck, 'unshaven, worn with lack of sleep and caked with dust. In the truck was a heap of straw as a bed, a can of stale water and a few tins of food. Close by were two wireless trucks and a few dispatch riders.' Mellenthin recalled how Rommel's forays cast a heavy responsibility on his junior staff officers, particularly the chief of operations section.

Archetypal pose of Rommel gazing over the battlefield from his command vehicle, in this instance a Horch 901 cabriolet.

A *Kriegsberichterstatter* (war correspondent) interviews Rommel (note the reel-to-reel tape recorder). 'I saw Rommel in a documentary film,' Goebbels wrote at the end of 1941. 'He talked for more than a quarter of an hour about his successes at the beginning of the year. Without any gesture he talked in a classic style, practically without correcting himself a single time. What he said and the way he said it, the play of his features and his whole appearance—all gave evidence of the greatness of an outstanding personality.' Shortly afterwards Goebbels could gloat that Rommel 'has truly become a ghost general. Today he is as well known in the USA as in London or Berlin, one of the few figures in the German Army to enjoy a worldwide reputation.'

The decorated *Kriegsberichterstatter* wears the Iron Cross, First and Second Class, and Panzer Assault Badge. The German propaganda magazine *Signal* waxed lyrical on the need for specialist war correspondents: '…experience has shown that the cleverest journalist and the most experienced broadcaster are not equal to their task unless they possess a soldierly spirit and knowledge of military matters…thus it is necessary that a German war correspondent today be a man of soldierly character and have a thorough grasp of his profession.'

The legend of the Desert Fox

Rommel's reputation began to grow in tandem with his easterly push across Libya. Nazi propagandists (disingenuously) claimed to have discovered that 'Rommel' was one of the many Arabic words for sand. Despite his failure to take Tobruk in April/May 1941—the first crisis on land for the Wehrmacht—his advance across a thousand kilometres of (worthless) desert quickly elevated his fame. Rommel's face soon began to grace the cover of both German and Allied illustrated magazines, while a 'flood of letters' began to arrive from adoring followers across the Third Reich. Touring the front lines, his adjutant noted on one occasion how Rommel was forced to flee a band of 'undisciplined soldier-photographers'. He had become, as von Esebeck described, 'The Lord of the Desert War'.

Rommel enjoyed his media success, and fame was a common theme in his letters home to his wife. By April 1941 he could boast to her that the 'press of the whole world' was following his deeds in the desert.

As Goebbels commented, 'there's hardly any other general so imbued with the vital importance of combat propaganda…he's a modern general in the best sense of the word.'

An official of the *Propagandaministerium* (Propaganda Ministry), *Leutnant* Alfred Berndt, was assigned to Rommel's staff, directing photographers, overseeing staged shots and composing valiant texts for magazines in Berlin. As German fortunes on the Eastern Front began to deteriorate in the closing months of 1941, *Reichspropagandaminister* Joseph Goebbels turned his attention to the 'Egyptian Front'. The Western Desert was the perfect counterfoil to the snowbound German Army following the failure of Operation Barbarossa.

After Tobruk fell in June 1942, Hans von Luck observed that Berlin 'didn't fail to put an undue value on Rommel's exploits, even though they treated our theatre of war in the desert as of only secondary importance.' Seizing upon Rommel's greatest victory, Goebbels coined the slogan: 'Our revenge for [the bombing of Cologne] is Tobruk.' Propaganda leaflets milking Rommel's renown were dropped in Egypt 'promising how the great hour will come…work for your freedom [from the British] as Rommel works for you.' Across the Atlantic, *Time* magazine rated him the 'best armoured-force general of World War II', and 'one of the great military commanders of modern times'; a *New York Times* headline censured how 'Rommel lectures the British on tactics.'

For a time, British troops even used the term 'a Rommel' to describe an impressive feat. Predictably, such complimentary exposure elevated Rommel to being the most recognised soldier in the Middle East during the war. According to one British observer, he was a 'general whose name, rightly or wrongly, was more of an admired household word among the Eighth Army than any held by our own.' British war correspondent Richard McMillan captured Britain's sense of recrimination in the wake of Tobruk's capitulation: 'We allowed the enemy in Libya to make every move—it was wait and see again…Rommel has become a bogey in the desert and the biggest bogey of all to many of the high-ups themselves. More often than I cared for I heard the words, "I wonder where Rommel's going to strike next"?'

Rommel's pervasive presence in the British Press helped cement the growing mythology. Britain's class system came to the fore with accusations hurled that Rommel would never have been promoted beyond sergeant had he served within the conservative ranks of the British Army.

Sensitive to the menace posed by the Rommel 'phenomenon', General Claude Auchinleck urged his officers not to be taken in by the cult of personality that had grown around their plucky adversary, warning how 'There exists a very real danger that our friend Rommel is becoming a kind of magician or bogey-man to our troops, who are talking far too much about him. He is no by no means a superman, although he is undoubtedly very energetic and able. Even if he were he a superman, it would still be highly undesirable that our men should credit him with supernatural powers. I wish you to dispel by all possible means the idea that Rommel represents something more than an ordinary German general. The important thing now is to see that we do not always talk of Rommel when we talk of the enemy in Libya. We must refer to "the enemy" or "the Germans" or "the Axis powers" and not always keep harping on Rommel.'

On 30 September 1942, Hitler presented Rommel with his field marshal's baton. That night Germany's Führer honoured his youngest Field Marshal at a rally at the Berliner *Sportpalast,* an event broadcast nationally to millions tuning in on their *Volksempfänger* (people's receiver) radios. The following day Goebbels gushed in his diary that Rommel is 'ideologically sound, [he] is not just sympathetic to the National Socialists. He is a National Socialist; he is a troop leader with a gift for improvisation, personally courageous and extraordinarily inventive. These are the kinds of soldiers we need. Rommel is the coming Supreme Commander of the Army.' He was also a distraction from the bloody war bogged down in the East, despite North Africa being a peripheral theatre, one holding the least strategic interest for Hitler.

Less than a month later, on the night of 23 October, the mooted 'supreme commander' was facing the greatest Allied offensive in North Africa to date. Suffering crippling loses, Rommel was forced to retreat or face annihilation. Infuriated, Hitler intervened, ordering his 'favourite general' to fight to the last man, 'to hold on, not to yield a step and to throw every weapon and every fighting man who can still be freed into the battle'; 'show your troops no other road than in victory or death.' Rommel estimated his losses at half of his infantry and almost half of his artillery. Only twenty-four of his tanks remained operational.

The *Panzerarmee Afrika's* daily situation report of 2 November highlighted how after 'ten days of uninterrupted fighting our own losses are exceptionally high, due to the overwhelming superiority of the enemy's infantry, tanks and artillery and the unremitting use he has made of his Air Force.' By the time permission to withdraw was received from Hitler and Italy's *Comando Supremo* on 4 November, the Axis forces were in full flight. Rommel's masterly retreat ended in Tunisia. On 8 March 1943 he left North Africa permanently. Two days later he was 'spontaneously' awarded the Diamonds to his Knight's Cross—a decoration bestowed to only twenty-seven officers. Distancing Rommel from the impending Axis capitulation in Africa, Goebbels was pleased to see that the Führer still possessed 'such a high opinion of Rommel'.

Rommel in the company of German and Italian naval personnel aboard a *Regia Marina* submarine in Bardia circa mid-November 1941. The boat was probably *Atropo*, one of three *Foca* (seal) class submarines. Launched in June 1937, *Atropo* survived the war and was scrapped in 1947. Mussolini was especially proud of his submarine fleet, which at the beginning of the war was the largest in the world after the Soviet Union.

All eyes on the front, in this case the British-held fortress of Tobruk.

Peering through a telescope, Rommel is framed by the loop antenna of a portable RF 3C, an Italian transmitter/receiver with a range of 20-50 km. Note the separate dry battery cases to the right. Distance, a U.S. wartime report concluded, 'is the principal problem encountered in desert communications. Radio is used extensively, as wire is laid only when there is time—an element often lacking in desert operations. Radio presents a unique problem of security, because radio communication is like shouting from place to place – all who can will listen.'

Generalmajor Karl Böttcher (far left), commander of the 21st Panzer Division, was another casualty of illness. Evacuated to Germany for treatment in February 1942, Böttcher's replacement, Generalmajor Georg von Bismarck, was killed by a mine in the Battle of Alam el Halfa on 31 August 1942. Böttcher survived the war. (Photograph taken on 29 November 1941).

An officer peers through a S.F. 14Z *Scherenfernrohr* (scissors periscope). Note Rommel behind.

As early as June 1941, Rommel's adjutant noted a deterioration in his general's health, a result of inadequate sleep and chronic exhaustion arising from a huge workload. Two months later in a meeting in Rome, Schraepler was shocked by Rommel's appearance. 'He did not look at all well: his voice was weak and he had suffered quite a serious heart attack. I tried to persuade him to rest for a few days. But he believed his return [to Africa] was necessary.'

Westphal wrote of the personal cost borne by Rommel in the desert: 'He was not only the soul but also the motive power of the North African war. Frugal and abstemious as he was, he would never have incurred the cardiac weakness which afflicted him in 1942 if it had not been for the continual over-activity to which he forces himself. His responsibility for the war theatre and for his troops lay heavy on him, and worry over the fate threatening his fatherland was an additional nagging distress.'

In August 1942 Rommel's personal physician certified that he was suffering from the effects of low blood pressure and was prone to fainting fits – a consequence of gastro-intestinal infections caused by excessive psychological and physical stress in combination with the harsh climatic extremes. A month later (on 22 September) he left for Wiener Neustadt to begin his treatment. Wrote Kesselring, 'Rommel was no longer the same daring leader. Continual, almost two-year long combat in hot climates coupled with endless friction with the Italians and the disappointment over the failure of his thrust toward Cairo had considerably damaged his health and, particularly, his nerves.' Goebbels later confided in his diary in 1943 that 'He must be a broken man due to his extended time in Africa. But one cannot let this fact become public because Rommel is, after all, the war idol of the Germans.'

Chapter Four
Towards the Nile

African oasis. The arrival of German troops in Libya signified an expansion of Nazi influence onto the African continent, an intervention romanticised in German newsreels. The only theatre of war on land since the fall of France was portrayed, as one commander in a Panzer regiment grumbled, with 'pictures of palm groves, oases, camels, donkeys, Arabs or pictures from Tripoli, Benghazi or Derna put in front of you and [you] think that is our world.'

A war correspondent at work; a 'sanitation' shovel at arm's reach. Hans Freiherr von Esebeck painted a colourful picture of the theatre, one in which the sun stood at the 'horizon like a milky disc in the haze of the morning clouds' and 'lifted the land slowly out of the enchantment of the night…On the remote road, which stretched over soft hills like a broad glittering shoelace, lay the fort of El Agheila, a tower, bulky, thick surrounded by walls of clay as if it…had been lifted from a tale in The Arabian Nights. Far off in the desert dust devils played in the morning wind, and the colours of the endless plain changed from the grey of first light to the yellow of day, flashing suddenly in a myriad of twinkling dew drops in which the silhouettes of the low camel-thorn bushes looked like ink blots…'

Shortly after arriving in Tripoli, Rommel ordered dummy tanks mocked-up on the chassis of Volkswagen *Kübel* Type 82s to 'enable us to appear as strong as possible and to induce the maximum caution in the British.' Alfred Gause later wrote how the '…fact that the Axis forces were always opposed by British in superior strength made Rommel inventive in the field of camouflage and deception, for example through diversionary attacks, and it was not without cause that he was called the "Desert Fox"… . Both sides practiced deception, the only difference being that the British endeavoured to camouflage their large numbers of tanks as trucks, whereas we endeavoured to simulate the presence of more tanks than we actually had.'

Italy's *Carro Armato* M14/41 was a 14-ton medium tank armed with a high velocity 47-mm gun and twin Breda 7.9 mm machine guns. A total of 752 were built. The Germans condemned the 'M' series as '*rollende Särge*' (rolling coffins). A German interpreter attached to the Italian XX Corps felt that the 'chance of surviving an attack in such a tank, not to speak of success, lay beyond the realms of courage which can morally be demanded.'

Rommel inspects an L3/35 tankette, originally known as CV 35, built by Fiat/Ansaldo. The Italian equipment, he wrote, made his 'hair stand on end'. Mussolini's light tanks were far more suited to fighting a war against a northern enemy across the Alps than against the British in the desert. To rectify the problem, Pietro Badoglio unsuccessfully tried to acquire some of the 700 tanks captured by the Germans in France, and for a period Italy even considered manufacturing the more reliable Pz.Kpfw. III under licence.

'The desert is definitely very much bleaker than I ever imagined,' Rommel's adjutant wrote home on 24 February 1941. 'We are not fighting in a developed region, where even if everything is destroyed, one can still find something useful, but we are in a desert of thousands of kilometres.' Trained to fight in Europe, Rommel and his men were faced with the challenge of mobility and rapidly lengthening supply lines in an environment largely devoid of cover and areas of concealment. The immense open spaces and monotonous landscape, so unlike Western Europe, also proved psychologically challenging for many Germans.

Unlike the Wehrmacht's European campaigns, in which soldiers could often requisition or capture food locally, the North African battlefield yielded nothing to sustain or support an army. Every item of food, fuel and ammunition was dispatched from Italy across the Mediterranean. This logistical headache was compounded by insufficient transport and lengthening supply lines across the desert. Halder wrote after the war: 'The German experiences in African desert warfare are made unique by the fact that the command and the troops were faced with a mission in no way either planned or prepared, and they entered into it completely without prior prejudices.'

Vehicles designed for European conditions suffered in the desert environment. Operating without appropriate air filters halved the average life of a tank engine – a problem exacerbated by the need to operate in low gear for extended periods. Although trucks could traverse much of the desertscape, many succumbed to broken springs and shock absorbers with spare parts not readily available. Wear and tear in the stony desert near El Alamein was particularly heavy.

The *Via Balbia* was frequently the object of British air attacks. Enormous distances confronted the *Afrikakorps* the further it pushed east towards Cairo. The distance from Brest-Litovsk on the Nazi-Soviet demarcation border in Poland, to Moscow, for example, was some 965 km (600 miles)—only half the distance from Tripoli to Alexandria.

 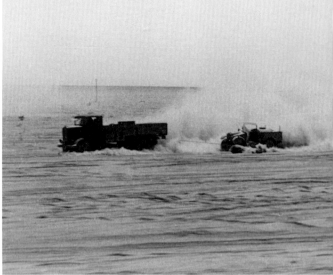

Hans Von Luck: In the absence of roads, 'normally one travelled in the desert only by compass, the most important instrument, carried by everyone…I learned to travel by compass and at the onset of darkness to find my way back to the battalion with mutual light signals. The reconnaissance trips into the desert held a great fascination for me.'

Desert convoy. Rommel believed that he had been posted to one of Germany's final theatres on land, ignorant of Hitler's forthcoming campaign to conquer the Soviet Union. Only in time did he come to realise that the desert was a sideshow dependent upon the Wehrmacht's fortunes in the East.

In early 1941 Gariboldi presented Rommel with a mobile office based on a Lancia 3Ro chassis. In a letter to Rommel's wife, Schraepler confided: 'I am very glad that your husband has an Italian caravan, which at least offers him some comfort and quiet, and protection against cold nights.'

Parking in a *wadi* (dry river bed) offered a degree of cover and protection from aerial attack in comparison to the flat surrounding terrain. In the event of a heavy downfall, however, a wadi could quickly flood. Hans von Luck recalled how 'the little wadis were filled in minutes with three-foot deep flash floods that carried all before them.' The photo was taken near Ras el Medauuar, Tobruk, on 18 April 1941.

A miscellany of German and captured British vehicles pictured on the *Via Balbia*. Mobile warfare across the desert, much like an open sea, was conducted with the aim of destroying enemy forces rather than occupying vast swathes of worthless land.

A post-war report by Bayerlein advised: 'In the desert all vehicles should carry shovels and planks or brush mats for use if they bog down in the sand…It is also advisable to furnish each car and some of the trucks with compasses, which should be so placed that they are at all times visible to the driver… passenger cars should be as light as possible.'

The organisation, width and depth of a desert route march plan was dependent upon the likelihood of enemy contact. When no engagement was expected, the width required for a division was roughly 500 meters, with a depth of 8 to 10 kilometres (5 to 6 miles). Noted a post-war commentary, 'In contrast to conditions in Europe, the assembly area in a desert can be far removed from the point of departure, since the lack of terrain obstacles permit vast areas to be covered in very short periods of time. As a result the troops can arrive at the point of departure very shortly before the beginning of the attack.'

Lending a hand. Rommel purportedly told the designer of the VW *Kübelwagen* ('bucket-car') Type 82, Dr. Ferdinand Porsche, that car had saved his life. Having inadvertently driven into a minefield, the lightweight vehicle failed to detonate any mines, unlike the trailing Horch vehicle, heavier and laden with luggage, which was destroyed.

The stylised palm tree with superimposed swastika stencilled on the door of this Auto Union/Horch model 901 officially became the insignia of the Deutsches Afrikakorps on 1 April 1941.

Portrait of a DAK officer. Note the dark *feldgrau* helmet, leather pistol holder, Iron Cross First Class and medal bar. The wearing of shorts was forbidden in combat zones, according to a post-war review of the theatre, since 'numerous soldiers were afflicted with exthyma [a bacterial skin infection] of the legs. After the wearing of long trousers or high boots had been enforced and small skin wounds carefully tended the number of these cases diminished very quickly. Rest was the most important prerequisite for a quick cure of the skin diseases.'

This Opel Blitz 3-tonner appears to be carrying drums of wine. Note the scales in the foreground and adjacent sacks of food.

The White House beside the Via Balbia served for a period as Rommel's headquarters. General Gerhard von Schwerin recalled him after the war 'seeing red' in April 1941 following the death of *Generalmajor* Heinrich von Prittwitz und Gaffron, the commanding officer of the Fifteenth Panzer Division recently arrived at Tobruk ahead of his division. Marching up to the White House to inform Rommel of the loss, it was the '…first time I saw him crack. He went pale, turned on his heel and drove off again without another word.'

Pumping water from a well. Wrote Fritz Bayerlein: 'A soldier arriving in a desert immediately adapts himself psychologically to the expected lack of water and with surprising speed accustoms himself to managing with the minimum quantity consistent with health.' Note the standard 'jerrycan' with white cross, a ready identification of water inside rather than fuel.

In May 1942, a captured British major of the 10th Hussars complained to Rommel that his men were not receiving adequate water rations. The latter replied that PoWs were receiving the same amount as German soldiers, himself included, of exactly half a cup a day. The captured officer then protested that, under the various Hague Conventions, if prisoners could not be properly provided for, then they should be allowed to return to their lines. Rommel momentarily took issue before replying, 'I agree that we cannot go on like this. If we don't get a convoy through tonight I shall have to ask General [Neil] Ritchie for terms.'

Schwere Panzerspähwagen (heavy reconnaissance armoured cars). From the left: Sd.Kfz. 231, Sd.Kfz. 232 and Opel Blitz truck. The cars featured dual steering and drive for all eight wheels. Both versions were introduced before the Polish campaign and saw service throughout the war.

Desert wanderer. The Wanderer Type W 23 touring car was produced in Germany by *Wanderer-Werke AG* from 1937 to 1942 as either a saloon, with body built by the Horch coachmaker, or as a convertible with body supplied by Gläser of Dresden. It sold for 6,450 Reichsmarks with 8,411 examples produced.

Cheerful comrades in arms outside Tobruk in May 1941. 'German and Italian soldiers', *Leutnant* Wilfried Armbruster penned in his diary, 'just light up when Rommel comes.' Luftwaffe *Generalfeldmarschall* Albert Kesselring wrote that the 'comradeship existing between Italian and German troops can be classified as good, even though at times honest embitterment at the attitude of Italian command and troops clouded the existing friendship.' According to Rainer Kriebel, 'It must be stressed that during the fighting around Tobruk not only German, but Italian troops as well, fought with great courage and persistence.'

Regarding his Italian allies, Rommel confided to his son Manfred that 'Certainly they are not good at war. But one must not judge everyone in the world by his qualities as a soldier: otherwise we should have no civilisation.'

German troops in North Africa frequently grumbled about their Italian allies. In a letter to his wife, a *Gefreiter* complained: 'Don't let anyone tell you that the Italians are soldiers. They are utterly useless. When they screw up we have to sort things out, costing us good German blood...' In a letter to Rommel's wife, his adjutant similarly blamed the Italians for the failure to seize Tobruk in mid-April 1941. 'We have far too few German forces and can do nothing with the Italians. They either do not come forward at all, or if they do, run at the first shot. If an Englishman so much as comes in sight, their hands go up. You will understand, Madam, how difficult this makes the command for your husband.' German military leaders, according to Siegfried Westphal, 'were not unaware of the weakness of the Italian forces, nor of the primitive nature of their equipment and training; they knew, moreover, that Italian industry was not in a position to supply the needs of the forces in a long war. Hitler on the other hand was convinced that Fascism had made the Italian soldier capable of extraordinary achievements...'

The outdated Italian 8-mm Mod. 1935 Fiat Revelli was a new, though not improved, version of the Mod. 1914 medium machine gun. Known as the 'knuckle-buster', the gas-operated, air-cooled gun proved difficult to handle, requiring lubricated ammunition and prone to premature exploding, or 'cooking off'. 'I have no sympathy,' von Mellenthin remonstrated, 'with those who talk contemptuously about the Italian soldier, without pausing to consider the disadvantages under which he labored.'

Rommel observing Italian troops, many shouldering rifles and spades. According to Kesselring, 'Rommel had acquired the habit of keeping his intentions secret from the [senior] Italians as long as possible, because he believed that the secrecy of his intentions was not sufficiently well-guarded. It is undoubtedly true that victory depends on absolute secrecy.'

Unaccustomed to protracted engagements and defeat, in April 1941 Rommel instigated 'feverish training' among his troops following their defeat at Tobruk. Culpability, in his eyes, lay with his men, as it had 'become only too evident' that their training in positional warfare was inferior to that of his enemy. This became a common theme. Rommel later justified the 1,200 casualties suffered in May fighting as a consequence of the switch from mobile to positional warfare. A German battalion commander protested in June that 'our people know nothing about the construction of defences. We have scarcely any exercise in this phase of warfare in our peacetime training. The junior commander does not realise that positional warfare is sixty per cent with the spade, thirty per cent with the field glasses, and only ten per cent with the gun.'

'The ground is rock hard', noted Hermann Aldinger, 'impossible to dig in; cover can only be made by heaping up rocks, and a canvas sheet is stretched out over them to provide some shelter from the scorching sun. This is why the soldiers don't wear much either – often just a pair of shorts. The lads are as brown as Negroes.' Note the camouflaged 3.7 cm Pak anti-tank gun.

The *schwerer Panzerfunkwagen* Sd.Kfz.263 8-rad (right) was a dedicated radio command vehicle based on the chassis of the Sd.Kfz.231/232 series. The crew of five comprised: driver, rear driver, two radio operators and commander. A single MG 34 machine gun was mounted on the front superstructure. Altogether, 240 of these vehicles were produced from April 1938 to April 1943.

Close-up of the Sd.Kfz.263 8-rad fixed superstructure.

The 5.8-ton Pz.Kpfw. I Ausf. B was armed with two MG 13 7.92-mm machine guns. A German wartime review of the Pz.Kpfw. I, which comprised a quarter of Rommel's initial armoured strength, dismissed it as too weak, too slow and totally unsuitable for desert operations.

An Sd Kfz 251/6 Ausf B. beside a captured British AEC 'Dorchester' armoured command vehicle. Writing in the *London Gazette* in 1948, General Harold Alexander (Claude Auchinleck's replacement as the commander-in-chief of Middle East Command in August 1942) praised Rommel as a 'tactician of the greatest ability' before challenging his 'strategic ability'. Alexander doubted 'whether he fully understood the importance of a sound administrative plan.' In his opinion, Rommel was happiest while directing a mobile force, though he was 'liable to overexploit immediate success without sufficient thought for the future.'

Oberst Erich Geißler (left) distinguished himself during Rommel's January 1942 offensive, at the capture of Tobruk on 20 June and the subsequent occupation of Mersa Matruh. He was awarded the Knight's Cross on 27 July 1942 for his actions while commanding the 200th Motorised Infantry Regiment, 90th Light '*Afrika*' Division. Geißler was evacuated from Africa due to illness on 1 May 1943.

The 5-man crew of a Pz.Kpfw. III Ausf. H pose for a photograph beside an immobilised Infantry Tank Mk II. Note the divisional emblem of the 15th Panzer Division to the right of the driver's visor.

A wounded radio operator (also the hull machine gunner) poses on his Pz.Kpfw IV Ausf. E. He wears the *Doppelfernhörer* b (Dfh. b) headphones with a *Kehlkopfmikrophon* b (Kmf. b) throat microphone. A wartime training manual specified that the 'radio operator operates the radio set under the orders of the tank commander. In action, when not actually transmitting, he always keeps the radio set at 'receive'. He operates the intercommunication telephone and writes down any radio messages not sent or received by the tank commander. He takes over the duties of the loader if the latter becomes a casualty.'

The short-barrelled 7.5 cm *Kampfwagenkanone* (KwK) gun was designed primarily as a close support weapon firing high explosive shells. Armour penetration using high explosive anti-tank and *Panzergranat-Patrone* 39 (armour-piercing capped) ammunition was limited due to the gun's low muzzle velocity. Note the supplemental armour plate bolted to the front of the superstructure.

Pz.Kpfw. III Ausf. G or H. On 30 April 1941, Rommel had 81 tanks available for deployment, only half of which were medium and heavy tanks—36 Mark IIIs and 8 Mark IVs.

Contrasting with these images was a diary entry penned by a tank battalion adjutant outside Tobruk five months later:

'There is a shortage of everything – of material, of reserve manpower. Our vehicles are on their bare rims. Poor rations have made more than 80 per cent of the regiment unfit to be sent forward...'

A mix of continental and *Afrikaner* headgear; the pith helmet is a South African pattern with the added *Wappen* (shield) containing the national colours of the Third Reich. Note the British aircraft 'kill' dated 16 May 1941, the opened vision ports to the left and the right of the main 5.0 cm KwK 38 L/42 canon, and the coaxial MG 34 machine gun.

A *Panzerbefehlswagen* (armoured command vehicle) Ausf. H (Type 7/ZW) from the 15th Panzer Division. Note the letter 'R', an abbreviation for Regiment, indicating that its belongs to the regimental staff. This Panzer would appear to be a Sd.Kfz. 266, equipped with FuG 6 and 8 radios. Note the large frame aerial for the long range FuG 8 resembling a handrail on the tank's rear deck. The three *Panzerbefehlswagen* variants, designated Sd. Kfz. 266, 267 and 268, differed according to the wireless equipment carried. All three had the prominent rail or loop aerial mounted over the rear deck.

Command tanks were characterised by extra radios, additional vision and pistol ports, including one in place of the machine gun on the front of the superstructure. A dummy gun is mounted in a fixed standard turret, which is bolted to the hull. Note the divisional pennant flying from the aerial.

The Pz.Kpfw. III was the most numerous German tank in North Africa. Writing of the fighting around Tobruk in November 1941, *Oberst* Reiner Kriebel wrote of the difficulty operating armour in the desert: 'The life of the tank engine is much shorter in the African theatre of war than in Europe. By this time the mechanical condition of the engine had deteriorated to such an extent that the majority of tanks were in urgent need of engine replacement…during the withdrawal the majority of damaged tanks and of these which had failed for mechanical reasons were abandoned to the enemy for lack of transport facilities.'

Panzerbefehlswagen. Note the medical company vehicles and distant explosions

Left to right: Phänomen Granit 25 H ambulance, Volkswagen *Kübel* Type 82 and Sd.Kfz. 250/3 half-track.

Tanks and tank destroyers. Note the five 'kill' rings on the barrel of the 8.8 cm Flak—Rommel's most effective tank destroyer, outranging all British tank guns.

A wartime U.S. intelligence bulletin noted that 'the object of the Germans is to knock out quickly as many of the antitank guns and foremost field guns as may be visible. When the German tank commander has decided to attack a position, his first objective has often been the British 25-pounders. By reconnaissance in tanks he first locates the British battery positions and makes his plans…He decides which battery to attack and he arranges to attack it from enfilade. His attack is made with 105-mm guns, the 88-mm dual-purpose guns, and both Mark III and IV tanks.'

Rommel: 'One of the first things I realized in motorised desert warfare was that here the speed of operations and the ability of the command to react quickly is a decisive factor. The troops must be able to operate in great haste and in perfect unity. Here one cannot be satisfied with any particular standard, but must always demand maximum performance, for the one who makes the greater effort is faster, and it is the faster side which wins battles in the desert.'

Heat, dust and often confusion. 'The contours of enemy vehicles,' noted *Hauptfeldwebel* Wilhelm Wendt (5th Panzer Regiment), 'were obscured to such an extent by the flickering heat that you could no longer tell what type of vehicle you had in front of you...'

German troops pictured outside Benghasi's Atiq Mosque, also known as *Al-Jami al-Kabir* (the Great Mosque), parts of which date back to the early fifteenth century. Berlin had first tried to raise Muslim support - a *jihad* - in its fight against Britain only weeks after the outbreak of the First World War. On 30 July 1914 Kaiser Wilhelm II declared: 'Our consuls and agents in Turkey, India and Egypt are supposed to inflame the Muslim regions to wild revolts against the British.' Should the plan succeed, then 'England shall lose at least India'. But as the Germans were to learn, success on the battlefield would play the biggest role in triggering a revolt across the Middle East against Britain. Despite having 30,000 men fighting in the Ottoman army, and bitter fighting against the British in Iraq, two attempts to seize the Suez Canal had failed.

An attempt to provoke a *jihad* was revisited during the Second World War. Nazi propaganda used shortwave radio to target the Egyptian populace after Tobruk capitulated. Stirring up opinion, a broadcast on 24 June questioned: 'Who of us Arabs has not been proud of Rommel? Who of us is not sympathising with him?' Via shortwave radio, the Grand Mufti of Jerusalem, Haj Amin al-Husseini, declared on 3 July: 'The Glorious victory secured by the Axis troops in North Africa has encouraged the Arabs and the whole East, and filled their hearts with admiration for Marshal Rommel's genius, and the bravery of the Axis soldiers. This is because the Arabs believe that the Axis Powers are fighting against a common enemy, namely the British and the Jews…' Hope for an anti-British rebellion in Egypt and neighbouring Palestine, however, quickly fell, in line with Axis fortunes, after El Alamein.

German *Kübelwagen* photographed in Benghazi April 1941.

124

One of several Sd.Kfz. 250/3 *leichter Funkpanzerwagen* used by Rommel, this one named after the mythical '*GREIF*' (Griffin). Production of the Sd.Kfz. 250 series began in June 1941 with 6,628 vehicles completed by the end of the war. Rommel was in his element when leading a battle group in person. *Oberst* Reiner Kriebel: 'Rommel's orders disregarded the weakness of the available troops and the difficulties of their supply problem. Reliance was placed on forces which in reality did not exist; tasks were allotted which were beyond the power of the formations, because these were doomed to immobility through shortage of fuel and ammunition.'

Parked next to Rommel's Sd.Kfz. 250/3 half-track (closest to the camera) are two Sd-Kfz. 251 half-tracks. The vehicle on the far left, an Ausf. C, carries the Italian word 'vinceremo' (we will win) on the frontal armour. The centre vehicle, a Sd.Kfz. 251/6 *Kommando-Panzerwagen* is an earlier Ausf. B model. Note the pennant on the mudguard denoting a divisional staff vehicle.

A rear view of Rommel's Sd.Kfz. 250/3 leichter *Funkpanzerwagen*. Note the added Jerrycan racks. The vehicle had a four-man crew with a single MG 34 machine gun with shield. Kesselring: 'It was a pleasure to observe Rommel's unique routine in the technique of desert command procedures.'

A pause in the fighting. Note the 4.7 cm Pak(t) (Sf). auf Pz.Kpfw. I Ausf.B or *Panzerjäger* I, the first German tank destroyer. Twenty-seven of these vehicles from *Panzerjäger Abteilung* 605, 5th Light Division, first arrived in Tripoli in March 1941. These vehicles, plus a small number of replacements, served as Rommel's only tank hunters until the battles for El Alamein in 1942.

Italian tankers pictured around a Fiat 508C Nuova Ballila 1100. *Regio Esercito* regulations stipulated that tank crewmembers stood between 1.50 and 1.54 metres tall.

German machine gunners shoulder their *Maschinengewehr* 34, or MG 34, 7.92-mm light machine guns. This advanced weapon could be fired from a bipod (pictured) or a heavier tripod for sustained fire. It was fed by either a belt or 75-round saddle drum magazine. Complex and expensive to produce, it was superseded by the *Maschinengewehr* 42, or MG 42.

Note the attempt to camouflage vehicles, though as a post-war review of German experiences in the desert concluded, 'Camouflage of works and obstacles by means of vegetation is altogether impossible in the desert.'

German 8 cm *Granatwerfer* 34, or 8 cm sGrW 34 (heavy grenade-launcher model 1934), and crew. The standard German heavy infantry mortar of the war, it could be broken into three loads: (i) baseplate, (ii) tube and (iii) bipod with the traversing, elevation and cross-levelling systems. Its reputation in Allied circles for rate of accuracy was more a reflection of crew training than of the weapon itself. Although classified as an 8 cm mortar, the actual caliber was 8.41 cm.

Rommel: 'Since the coastal road was closed by the British in Tobruk, all supply traffic for the troops east of Gambut had to move through the terrain around Tobruk. The old trails which had been marked for use in this terrain were so worn out that they could only be traversed with difficulty. At many points it was found to be utterly insurmountable, for small vehicles and trucks could only be driven through by taxing their motors to the utmost. If a column of trucks managed to cover the distance around Tobruk within a day, this was considered an excellent performance, and the distance was only roughly seventy kilometres. I therefore exerted all my influences in urging the top level Italian authorities to build a road bypassing Tobruk.' According to Bayerlein, 'Five metres wide, the road was ballasted though not asphalted.' In light of the extremely primitive equipment available, the result was considered 'remarkable'.

The 45-mile (70 km) *strada dell'Asse* or *Achsenstrasse* skirted the perimeter of besieged Tobruk. Constructed with 'great enthusiasm' in some ten weeks, the road opened on 9 August 1941. The British later rechristened the road 'Democracy Lane'.

According to Heinz Schmidt, 'We drove along the Axis road one day when it was nearing completion, and he [Rommel] was genuinely pleased with the accomplishment of the Italian road builders…Rommel called on a fat Italian major who was commanding one of the road construction battalions. "Tell him, Dr Franz, that I am extremely pleased with the excellent work that has been accomplished." The rotund major's face beamed with pleasure at the compliment…'

Under an air attack from British bombers, September 1941. Hans-Joachim Schraepler (16 May 1941): 'The fighting in the desert is really particularly bitter. We don't think anyone at home can imagine it.'

Allied observers in North Africa reported four principles of German armoured attack: (i) the primary role of the tank is to kill infantry; (ii) the machine gun is therefore an important weapon of the tank; (c) the tank can be successful only when it is used in conjunction with all arms; (d) tanks must be used in mass.

A burning Marmon-Herrington Mk III. South Africa produced 2,630 of these armoured cars in 1941-42.

British Universal Carrier. Note the gas mask and distinctive Caunter Scheme camouflage, a term used today to describe the disruptive colour scheme used by the British devised by Brigadier J.A.L 'Blood' Caunter of the 4th Armoured Brigade, using slate silver grey and light stone in a horizontal splinter pattern. This particular Carrier, No. T8313, was built by Nuffields in 1939. The '79' painted on a green square on the mudguard indicates that it belonged to an armoured brigade's motor battalion.

German troops first encountered the British Infantry Tank Mk II, or Matilda II, during the Battle of France. Bulletins were subsequently published from tests on captured vehicles giving the effective ranges of anti-tank guns: 200 metres with the 3.7 cm Pak firing Pzgr.40 ammunition; 600 metres with the 5.0 cm Pak 38 firing Pzgr.40 ammunition and 1,500 metres from the 8.8 cm Flak 18/36 firing 8.8 cm Pzgr. All German weapons with calibres of 20 mm or higher were measured in centimetres.

Nevertheless, the immunity of the tank to weapons smaller than the 8.8 cm Pak was a nasty surprise to many, including the Panzer battalion commander court-martialled by Rommel for his weakness in the fighting at Halfaya Pass on 27 May 1941 when nine Matildas held off some 160 Axis tanks. Note the two penetration holes in the thick frontal armour.

The diary of the 8. *Maschinengewehr Bataillon* (8th Machine Gun Battalion) recorded the ineffectiveness of the 3.7 cm Pak against Matilda tanks: 'Its shells just bounce off the tank's thick armour, only a lucky shot in its tracks or turret bearings have any effect. So they rumble on to within 100 yards of our position, halt and then knock out our Paks one by one. We watch bitterly as one gun after another stops firing. Even individual acts of gallantry cannot help in this situation. Gunner Blank of 7 Company is still firing on a Matilda at five yards' range: no good. The steel colossus rolls on over him and his gun…our surgeon has to amputate both legs on the battlefield because they are just pulp. Later he died of his injuries.'

Note the solid shot shell in the foreground, a round dependent upon kinetic energy to punch through armour plate.

The most heavily armoured tank in North Africa at this time. Although the Matilda II was protected by 78 mm (3.07 in) of frontal armour, Rommel was puzzled by its main armament and ammunition, commenting: 'They were only supplied with solid, armour-piercing shell. It would be interesting to know why the Mark II was called an infantry tank when it had no HE ammunition with which to engage the opposing infantry. It was also…far too slow. In fact, its only real use was in a straight punch to smash a hole in a concentration of material.'

Cleanly penetrated British armour. The heavier German tanks, the Pz.Kpfw. III and IV, had the distinct advantage of face-hardened armour – a metallurgical advance that helped to deflect the kinetic energy of solid-shot projectiles. A number of DAK tanks also had additional face-hardened armour plates bolted onto the hull front and superstructure of the tank, affording even greater protection. The British and Italian tanks, by comparison, were protected by less effective homogeneous armour. The standard British anti-tank gun, the 2-pounder, could only fire solid-shot armour-piercing projectiles, which tended to disintegrate on striking face-hardened armour.

Knocked-out Matilda, possibly a victim of the carefully sited 8.8 cm guns at Halfaya Pass during the Battle of Sollum (15-17 June 1941).

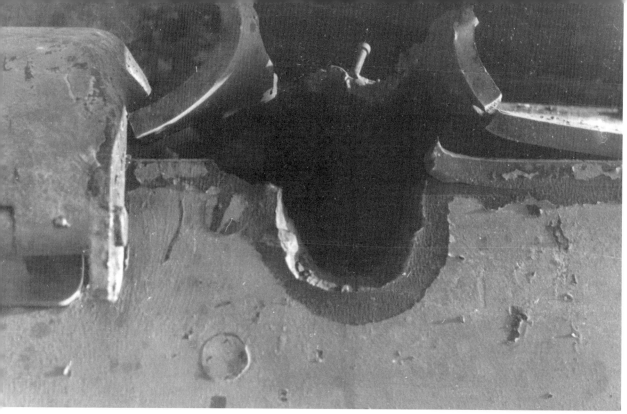

Close-up inspection of pierced and damaged British armour. German armour-piercing ammunition, in all calibres of 37mm and above, contained high explosive with a time delay fuse. In striking a British tank, penetration was frequently associated with wounding of the crew, irreparable damage or fire. It was not until 1942 that British authorities investigated the cause of the fires, leading to the installation of armoured bins to protect ammunition.

This knocked-out British Cruiser Mark IV was also armed with the 2-pounder gun. German forces were familiar with the tank from the French campaign and the nearly 100 vehicles captured on the Allied retreat to Dunkirk. Renamed the Pz.Kpfw. Mk.IV 744(e), captured examples served in the Soviet Union and the Balkans.

Successor to the Matilda, the Infantry Tank Mk III or Valentine was a vehicle of exceptional endurance in the desert. The British 2-pounder projectile it fired relied entirely upon residual kinetic energy to destroy a German tank. Since the ammunition carried by a Pz.Kpfw. III or IV was stored in armoured bins, with the fuel protected by an armour plate firewall, seldom did a 2-pounder AP shot result in irreparable damage or the complete destruction of a German tank.

Close up view of combat damage to a British Valentine, apparently from a mine and anti-tank projectiles.

The Italian Fiat SPA *Dovunque* ('anywhere') 35 6 x 4 was specifically designed for use in North Africa. Production continued under German control after the Italian armistice in September 1943 with 307 trucks delivered to the Wehrmacht.

Two Horch 901 cabriolets, the pennanted one possibly Rommel's, parked in the relative safety of a depression.

Auto Union/Horch 901 Type 40 (one spare wheel stored inside the car body). Looking at the camera is *Generalmajor* Artur Schmitt, commander of fortress Bardia, which surrendered to the British on 2 January 1942. Schmitt spent the remainder of the war in Canada as a prisoner of war.

Deliberation: Walter Neumann-Silkow, Ludwig Crüwell and Hans Hecker (*Pionier-Führer der Panzergruppe Afrika*). Note the armoured car in the background, likely a Sd.Kfz. 222 because of the turret screens.

An Opel Blitz Type W39 with a body built by Ludewig, an Essen-based company that manufactured specialised omnibuses for the Wehrmacht beginning in 1939 (model W 39).

Field communications; note the handset of the *Feldfernsprecher* 33 (field telephone 33).

The cover of the June 1941 edition of *Der Adler*, featuring Ju 87s in North Africa

The distinctive gull-wing shape of the German Junkers Ju 87 or Stuka (from *Sturzkampfflugzeug*, meaning 'dive bomber').

A former Stuka pilot recalled his arrival into North Africa: 'Derna landing ground: nothing but sand and stones as far as the eye could see. Here nothing grew – no trees to provide welcome shade, no bushes, not even weeds…'

This photograph by *PK Kriegsberichter* Ernst Zwilling shows Rommel and staff observing a Stuka bombardment.

A captain in the 115th Panzer Grenadier Regiment recounted the bombing during Rommel's 1942 assault on Tobruk: 'Then a full throated roar: Our Stukas were approaching. Carefully we laid out the identification strips we bought with us. Before now we had been given a taste of our own Stuka bombs. The battle was on…The Stukas dropped their noses and swooped down over our heads. They plunged at the enemy perimeter. Bombs screamed down and crashed into the minefield. Rommel had thought up a new trick in the desert. He was not bombing the defenders, but blasting a way through the minefield…The Stukas, their bomb bays empty, their motors roaring, swung back low over our heads. They flew without interference, for the RAF had been driven off the Gambut airfield, and the Luftwaffe had no *Huren-Kähne* [Hurricanes] to harass them.'

A senior chaplain with the Second South African Division afterwards described the terrifying effect of being dive-bombed. 'Down they whistled, always, it seemed to the anxious watching and prostrate observer, directly at him: then there was apparent a little curtsy in the bomb's flight—a strange illusion of tensed nerves—and it passed up and over to explode twelve or twenty-five feet away.' A 1943 British study on the effect of enemy weapons on the morale of 300 British soldiers wounded in North Africa found that the Stuka was the 'most disliked' weapon; moreover it was 'disliked to an extent out of all proportion to its real effectiveness'. Of the 176 men who had experienced dive-bombing, only nine per cent were wounded. In contrast, sixty per cent of troops who had faced a German 8.8 cm gun had been wounded.

Examining a downed fighter aircraft. Germany's highest scoring fighter pilot in the desert was *Hauptmann* Hans-Joachim Marseille, nicknamed the 'Star of Africa'. Serving with *Jagdgeschwader* 27, Marseille recorded his highest tally on 1 September 1942 when he claimed 17 Allied fighters during three combat sorties. Before his death on 30 September, aged 22, Marseille had flown 382 sorties and shot down 158 enemy aircraft, including 101 P-40 Kittyhawks, 30 Hurricanes, 16 Spitfires and 4 bombers – the highest such achievement by an Axis pilot against the Western Allies. Italian engineers later constructed a small pyramid at the site of Marseille's death.

Fort Capuzzo (*Ridotta Capuzzo*) was an Italian-built fort near the Libyan-Egyptian border that changed hands numerous times over the course of the Desert War.

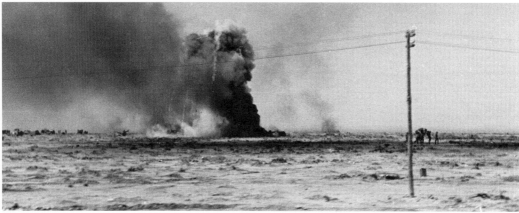

Bombardment. A British NCO wrote of Rommel's firepower: I 'have seen enough in the last two weeks to become a most ardent pacifist. The other campaign was a child's game compared to this. We are all in a state known as 'bomb happy' – the effect of continuous shelling, bombing, and strafing, they even keep it up during the night which isn't funny. It's a lousy feeling to wake up with tracer bullets buzzing around one; 'fraid I feel rather shaky…I've seen and known the filthiest sights here.'

An explosion photographed out to sea. Rommel's adjutant recorded an incident on 31 May 1941 when a cargo vessel was spotted on the horizon. Luftwaffe aircraft subsequently bombed the ship, which caught fire, followed by a 'detonation more powerful than I had ever heard…obviously an ammunition carrier.'

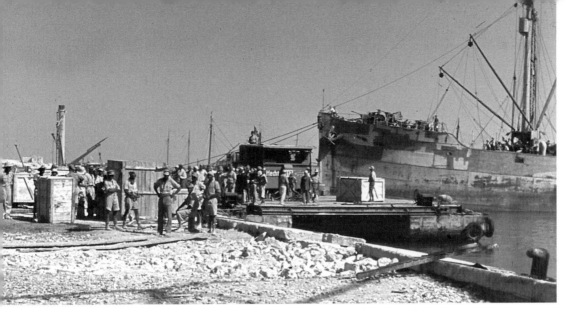

Rommel, his subordinate officers acknowledged, showed little initial interest in his supply situation, which he later declared was 'absolutely fundamental'. Barely months into the campaign (8 May 1941), Schraepler protested about the growing supply/transport problem: 'There are enormous difficulties with supplies. Sometimes this is missing, sometimes that. We always lack loading capacity. A large quantity of supplies has arrived in Tripoli, but we could not transport it.'

The Axis supply lines were much shorter than those of the British, but virtually every Italian convoy to North Africa faced the threat of attacks from British aircraft and submarines based at Malta. This predicament frustrated Rommel, who in turn blamed his Italian allies and German quartermasters. But as General Paulus informed OKH, 'The crux of the problem in North Africa is not Tobruk or Sollum, but the organisation of supplies.' After a briefing from Paulus, Halder documented Rommel's culpability: 'Situation in North Africa unpleasant. By overstepping his orders Rommel has brought about a situation for which our present supply capabilities are insufficient. Rommel cannot cope with the situation.'

Some 1,210 Axis convoys plied the Mediterranean during the battles for the Western Desert. Italian ships carried a total of 2,345,381 tons of materiel to Libya. Despite frequent British attacks, only 14% or 315,426 tons was actually lost. Of the 206,402 troops carried by Italian vessels, often warships, to Africa, 17,204 or 8.5% were lost at sea (though many were rescued). These figures do not include men and materiel shipped in German vessels or airlifted by the Luftwaffe.

An Italian submarine departs Bardia after delivering sixty tons of fuel. According to Kesselring, 'It was obvious that Rommel paid more attention to the situation in the field, although he should have known that supply was going to be the decisive factor in the African Theatre of Operations.'

A freighter pictured at Bardia. Lower Bardia, seen in the foreground, contained a number of military buildings, barracks, storehouses, a pumping station, harbour office facilities and a small jetty. The harbour provided shelter to seaplanes and an achorage for vessels up to 4,000 tonnes.

Supplies brought by sea from Italy to Bardia were ferried ashore by lighter in fair weather. Hundreds of fuel containers are seen here on the beach.

Bardia. Rommel's prioritisation of manoeuvre over assured supply came to a head after the capture of Tobruk in June 1942 during his final abortive push into Egypt. (The Italian tractor is possibly a Landini velite)

Urgently needed supplies. In light of the *Afrikakorps'* chronic transport shortage, General Kirchheim at one point even suggested to General Halder that camels could be used to ease the crisis.

Leading this command column is a Sd.Kfz. 251/3 or 251/6 medium armoured semi-track radio command vehicle, followed by a *mittlerer geländegängiger Personenkraftwagen* (medium cross-country passenger car) Kfz. 12, type 901, car body type 40. To the left is a *le. gp. Beobachtungs-Kraftwagen* (light armoured observation motor vehicle), Sd.Kfz. 253 featuring an unusual additional frame antenna and the tactical sign of the 21st Panzer Division.

Photographed against the backdrop of burning British stores is a *Funk-Betriebskraftwagen* (radio motor-vehicle) Kfz. 17, identifiable by the frame antenna and rear radio mast.

A British Universal Carrier, or Bren 731(e) in German nomenclature, leads a staff column from the 21st Panzer Division.

Across the barbed wire can be seen a 5 cm PaK 38, a captured British light 15-cwt truck and a Volkswagen *Kübel* Type 82.

Fixed defences, possibly pictured near the Libyan-Egyptian frontier.

German engineers prepare to bridge the anti-tank ditch surrounding Tobruk in a series of propaganda photographs. Note the Pz.Kpfw. II in the background.

The wooden bridge is successfully moved into position and tested. By June 1942, however, the anti-tank ditch ahead of the Indian Second Mahratta Light Infantry, who bore the brunt of Rommel's assault in the southeast sector of the perimeter, had deteriorated to the extent that it was only a nominal obstacle that 'would hardly have interfered with the progress of a garden roller'. The light truck from a medical company is a Ford Type 01 Y with a South-African-built body.

Stores from captured warehouse under new ownership; the closest truck is a Ford G917T.

A greatcoated Rommel pictured before a 1941 Ford NAAFI/EFI mobile canteen truck between Tobruk and Sidi Omar. The British EFI (Expeditionary Force Institutes) provided NAAFI (Navy, Army and Air Force Institutes) goods in war zones. The tartan scarf he wears was possibly a present from his illegitimate daughter Gertrud (born on 8 December 1913 at Weingarten, a town in Württemberg, in the District of Ravensburg).

Booty (boxes of British evaporated milk and pilchards above) was always a welcome addition to the monotonous diet of an army increasingly incapacitated by illness. 'How pitiful our equipment is in every respect, compared with the British,' Colonel Maximilian von Herff complained. 'Just look at the supplies they get—mineral water, tinned preserves and fruit, things we sorely lack. This lack is becoming increasingly evident from the damage to our youngsters' health as the days get hotter. Even our 25-year-olds are already losing their teeth and their gums just won't stop bleeding…'

Italian Paolo Caccia-Dominioni wrote of the 'entire villages' of warehouses captured at Tobruk: 'There were stacks of tinned beer; huts bursting with pure white flour, cigarettes, tobacco and jam; gallons of whiskey; priceless tinned foods of all kinds; and tons of khaki clothing—that magnificent khaki, which looked so heavy and was so light and cool to wear.'

Rommel, aboard a Sd.Kfz. 250/3 command vehicle, looks ahead across the desertscape. Note the shielded MG 34 machine gun with anti-aircraft sight.

Chapter Five
Kriegsgefangene (PoWs)

Wounded British PoWs. Rommel is alleged to have incinerated Hitler's *Kommandobefehl* (Commando Order), issued on 18 October 1942, upon receiving it. The controversial directive called for 'all men operating against German troops in so-called Commando raids in Europe or in Africa, are to be annihilated to the last man.' After the war former general Hans Speidel and Admiral Friedrich Ruge claimed that Rommel had instilled a sense of chivalry in soldiers, whom he urged to adhere to the 'laws of humanity'.

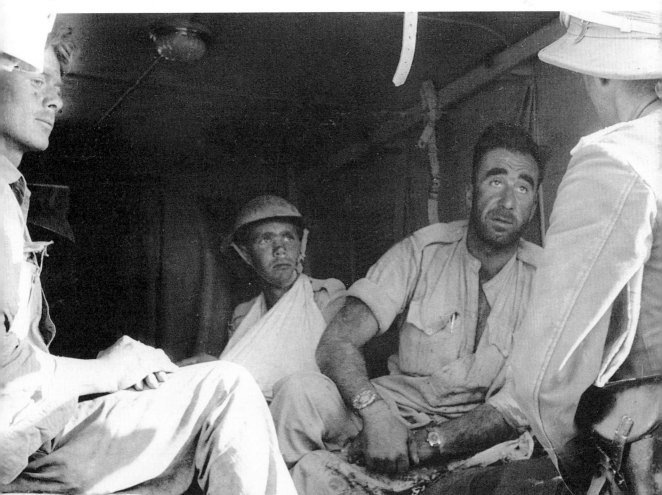

Writing after the war, Field Marshal Sir Claude Auchinleck wrote of Rommel's graciousness towards prisoners of war: '…this used to be called chivalry: many will now call it nonsense and say that the days when such sentiments could survive a war are past. If they are, then I, for one, am sorry.'

Major General Michael Gambier-Parry photographed following the fall of Mechili on 8 April 1941 (The other British officer, seen wearing sunglasses, is Colonel George Younghusband). The engagement, Rommel could boast, 'was a coup... Their [British] troops were taken completely by surprise and probably were deceived as to our true strength... It was principally our speed that accounted for this victory. Gambier-Parry had earlier taken command of the depleted British 2nd Armoured Division on 12 February 1941 (the same day Rommel arrived in Tripoli) following the death of Major General Justice Tilley. In 2015, Gambier-Parry's granddaughter revealed another twist to the Desert Fox goggle saga, namely that the captured general had given Rommel the British goggles – 'Eyeshields, Anti-Gas, Mk I-that were to adorn his peaked cap throughout the desert campaign.' Over dinner, Gambier-Parry had complained to his German host of having had his hat stolen by a German soldier. An incensed Rommel saw that it was returned to its owner. When he spied Gambier-Parry's goggles, the latter agreed that he could keep them.

British prisoners of war were transported across the Mediterranean to camps in Italy or Germany. The journey could be hazardous with several transports attacked by British aircraft or submarines: On 14 February 1942, *HMS P38* sank *Aristo* with the loss of 135 PoWs; on 13 October *Unruffled* (P46) sank *Loreto* with 100 Indian PoWs killed; on 13 November Sahib (P212) sank *Sicilian* with 830 PoWs killed.

Hans-Otto Behrendt, a senior member of Rommel's intelligence staff, wrote of the value of intelligence gleaned from PoWs: 'Soldiers who become prisoners of war mostly come directly from the battlefield. They have been taking part on the other side. They have still to get over the shock of being captured by the time they are interrogated about details interesting to us. Intelligence officers then put together the results like pieces in a jigsaw puzzle, even though they may seem unimportant to the prisoner. Thus these interrogations provide a fertile source of intelligence. Uniform badges are mute proof of what unit the prisoner belongs to, particularly valuable when – as was normally the case with British prisoners – the statements were more than scanty. The British had in fact briefed their troops meticulously on what to expect when taken prisoner, whereas in the German Army it was not customary to dwell on the possibility of being captured. The British PoW knew what interrogations they would be subjected to and what questions they would be asked. An excellent British guide, with poignant title *The Answer to this is Silence*, was therefore translated and made available as an instructional leaflet to each member of the forces engaged in Africa to keep with his paybook on 14 May 1942: It instructed him that even as a prisoner of war he should endeavour to do his duty. When interrogated all he had to state according to international convention was his name, rank, date and place of birth, and place of residence. To any other question he should simply reply: "I cannot answer that." The enemy would respect this stance. A free tongue could mean death to his comrades. He should also beware of agents in German or Italian uniforms pretending to be fellow prisoners, and also of hidden microphones.'

British prisoners congregated around a Ford G 917/997 T (left) and Borgward 3-tonner (right).

Name, rank and number…British prisoners are interrogated.

Victor and vanquished. After the fall of Tobruk, a furious Rommel demanded to know why General Hendrik Klopper had destroyed trucks plus stocks of water and petrol. When the South African failed to answer, Rommel responded with the threat that his captured troops would have to walk to Tripoli. 'My men are now prisoners of war and must be treated as such', Klopper retorted. 'Do what you want with me.'

The North African campaign is viewed by many today as an 'honourable' one, an almost gentlemanly conflict as opposed to the far larger ideological struggles contested on European soil. Rommel, for one, insisted that prisoners of war share the same rations as his own men. Following the fall of Tobruk in June 1942, a group of South African officers demanded to be segregated from the blacks. This request was turned down by Rommel, who pointed out that the blacks are South African soldiers too: 'they wear the same uniform and they have fought side by side with the whites. They are to be housed in the same PoW cage.'

Chapter Six
Beutefahrzeuge

Rommel, standing in his Sd.Kfz. 250/3 armoured half-track, pauses on the road to Cairo opposite a column of captured British vehicles. The first truck is a CMP Chevrolet 60-cwt Type C 60 L (Type 12 cab) captured by the Italians and armed with a 20 mm Breda AA gun model 35. The truck in the background could be a Ford Type 01. Axis forces, from the outset of the campaign in North Africa, were beset by a shortage of transport. A month into the fighting Rommel's adjutant described in a letter home that 'our destroyed vehicles are being replaced by excellent British cars, so that some German units will not be recognised as German, and one might think that there are English here. Besides, our men can barely be identified, covered by dirt and dust.' A report by Major Ernst-Otto Ballerstedt (115th Motorised Infantry Regiment) in August 1941 recommended that drivers should have a good knowledge of all vehicle types in North Africa, including British models with a view to using captured examples.

A pause in the flat and featureless desert. During the fighting for Mechili on 7-8 April 1941, German troops captured three 4 x 4 British AEC 'Dorchester' armoured command vehicles belonging to Lieutenant Generals Richard O'Connor and Phillip Neame, and Major General Michael Gambier-Parry. Rommel kept two of these 'Mammut' (Mammoth) vehicles: one for himself dubbed 'Max'; 'Moritz' was used by *Generalleutnant* Ludwig Crüwell; the third vehicle was allocated to General Johannes Streich of the 5th Light Division.

Senior staff officers in front of their appropriated armoured command vehicle, 'Moritz'. Schraepler (second from the left) died in an accident in December 1941 when he was run over by a *Mammut*.

The vehicle christened 'Moritz' was named after a character in a popular children's story written by Wilhelm Busch. Seen here still carrying its original camouflage scheme, it was allocated the number plate WH-819834. German war correspondent Fritz Lucke described the vehicle as a 'an armoured box as big as a bus, on giant balloon tires as big and fat as the undercarriage wheels of a Junkers transport plane. The walls are windowless and painted in blue-grey camouflage shades. Only the driver and his co-driver have windshields, protected behind armoured visors.'

According to former general Alfred Gause: Rommel 'never used a command tank, considering this type of vehicle too slow and not manoeuvrable enough when under fire. He did occasionally ride a captured British mammoth type command tank [sic], but never when leading an attack.'

One of Rommel's Mammuts leads a *mittlerer Kommandopanzerwagen* Sd. Kfz. 251/6 armoured commander's half-track. Note the distinctive radio antenna.

Other vehicles in this series of photos include VW Type 82 *Kübelwagen*, a Pz.Kpfw. I and Auto Union/Horch 108 Kfz 70 personnel carrier.

According to Heinz W. Schmidt, Rommel's aide-de-camp, Rommel spotted a pair of British sand and sun goggles inside this captured vehicle at Mechili: 'He took a fancy to them. He grinned, and said "Booty – permissible, I take it, even for a General". He adjusted the goggles over the gold-braided rim of his peak cap. Those goggles for ever after were to be the distinguishing insignia of the "Desert Fox".' He recalled a scene where Rommel, 'looking like a U-boat commander on his bridge' was 'perched high up on the edge of the *Mammut's* "sunshine roof".' Rommel's aide, Hermann Aldinger, wrote how the 'ACV rolls as though we are on the high seas and we are thrown about inside however tight we hold on. The general and I climb up and sit on the roof—there are three exit hatches on top—and keep a look out on all sides, because enemy aircraft can be a real menace.' Schmidt detailed an incident when a driver of the vehicle was badly injured during an air attack, one of many instances where Rommel escaped unscathed while those next to him were killed or injured. Unperturbed, Rommel took over the wheel, driving throughout the night. Rommel's 'Max' was put out of action in September 1941.

Rommel, according to Alfred Gause, was a keen hunter and excellent marksman. 'His close affinity with nature had sharpened his sense for terrain appreciation and his orientation ability to a remarkable degree. Frequently he would drive day and night through the trackless desert without maps, using a compass only rarely to check his direction.'

Under new ownership. The Matilda's German designation was *Infanterie-Kampfpanzer* Mark II 748(e). Held in high regard by the Germans, Hans-Joachim Schraepler lauded the tank in June 1941 as the 'heaviest and strongest in the world.'

Italian officers alongside a Fiat 508 C/1100 *Militare* with either a Fiat 1100 or 1500 in the background. Fiat was Italy's largest wartime vehicle manufacturer. Note the captured South African Marmon-Herrington Mk II armoured car, marked '73'.

Another captured Marmon-Herrington Mk II in DAK service, this time minus turret in an observation role. British crews often rearmed their vehicles with captured enemy weapons. Rommel's driver pictured here is Hellmut von Leipzig.

Inspecting a captured British 6-inch 26-cwt howitzer. A weapon dating from the First World War, the original wooden spoked wheels were replaced with steel-rimmed wheels and pneumatic tyres during the interwar period. In German service the gun received the designation: 15.2 cm sFH 412(e).

Captured British QF 25-pounder gun/howitzers. The term 'Quick Firing' originated because the brass cartridge case enabled rapid loading compared to bag charges and was automatically ejected when the breech was opened. Until Britain adopted the metric system, all artillery was designated by the weight of the projectile, in this instance the weight of the high explosive shell. The German term for the designation of captured weapons and other material was: *Kennummer für Beutegerät.* In this instance the weapon was designed by the calibre of the gun: 8.76(8.8) cm, K for cannon, then the *Kennummer* 281, FK 281(e), and 'e' for England.

A captured Morris Commercial C8 FAT (Field Artillery Tractor), commonly known as a 'Quad', towing a 25-pounder and artillery trailer or 'limber'. According to a former British bombardier: 'The Quads were a curious stubby vehicle purpose built for towing a gun. Four wheel drive so that it could get out of difficult situations. It had a flap on the roof so you could put your head out and you could see where you were going and direct the driver…It had the unfortunate impression that it looked like an armoured vehicle because it had flat slabby sort of sides. I think it gave people a feeling of security that was totally false – but it wasn't armoured at all.'

An early Mk II model Quad. Note the swastika painted on the door, dual limbers and jerrycan rack above the door, apparently a German field upgrade. Italian formations also used the 25-pounder, such as one battalion in the 'Trento' Division with twelve guns that fought at El Alamein. The 25-pounder's Italian designation was Obice da 88/27 PB, the 'PB' standing for Preda Bellica or war booty.

The 25-pounder, the standard British field gun of the Second World War, fired 'separate' or two-part ammunition comprising a propelling charge (usually in a brass cartridge case and separate projectile). Probably the DAK's deadliest enemy in the desert, the number 210 fuse was available at El Alamein for air burst use. This was deemed particularly useful in combating German 8.8 cm gun crews.

A July 1942 DAK report signed by General Walter Nehring praised British artillery for its 'great versatility, quick to open fire…with trained observers who fired quickly and with manoeuvrability'. According to a former British gunner, 'if a high explosive 25-pounder shell hits it's going to blow the track off and the tank will slew and stop. That means you can put another one into it, bang one into the back and he'll explode and brew up.'

The British 'Trailer, Artillery, No 27' had a capacity of thirty-two 25-pounder rounds stored in sixteen trays. A former British bombardier recalled that the '25 pounder [projectile] fragmented into tiny pieces which never got much above knee high as it spread. So it was a great killer and as an artilleryman looking for something that will kill it was an efficient projectile.'

Another British limber is examined; note the Italian aircraft wreckage in the background. The gunners' personal kit was usually carried under a tarp on the front of the trailer. Difficult to back and manoeuvre, the limber disappeared from use after the 25-pounder became obsolete.

A British Vickers-Armstrong QF 2-pounder anti-tank gun in Italian Service. Towed behind a truck on two rubber-tyred wheels, it was lowered onto three outriggers for firing.

British WOT2 and possibly an Austin K30 in the background. British *Beutefahrzeuge* (captured vehicles) included a variety of 15-cwt, 30-cwt and 3-ton trucks. Nearly 80 per cent of the DAK soft-skin vehicle fleet was comprised of captured models by the time of the Axis capitulation in Tunisia in May 1943.

A miscellany of vehicles from both sides. Left to right: Chevrolet Type 1532 ambulance, Sd.Kfz. 222 armoured car, possibly an Italian tractor Spa Type TL 37 with a staff trailer, a *mittlerer Einheits*-PKW and a Horch 901 cabriolet bearing the DAK pennant.

Two Ford Type 01 Y trucks bookending a VW Type 82 *Kübelwagen*. Note the lifted German Tellermines in the foreground and several British anti-tank mines.

Two captured Chevrolet 6-cwt or 3-tonners of the 1500-series, Type 1543 X 2 or CC 60 L.

Captured Ford 01 Y 15 cwt, likely a former South African vehicle.

Under the swastika—a Canadian Military Pattern (CMP) Ford 60-cwt Type F 60 with No. 12 pattern cab. The two-part radiator grille on this model, in which the upper part opened with the bonnet, was known as an 'Alligator' cab. CMP trucks were manufactured to British specifications for use in Commonwealth armies as well as being sent to the Soviet Union. Rommel appreciated that traditional non-motorised transport had no place in the desert, 'for the side which makes the greater effort is the faster, and the faster side wins the battle.'

Another snapshot of Rommel's captured transport. Pictured in the centre is a Chevrolet 60-cwt Type C 60 L with a No 12 pattern cab. Far right is a captured CMP Chevrolet 60-cwt Type CC 60 L. Sandwiched between the Chevrolets is possibly a Bedford 3-tonner Type OY. Far left is either a Chevrolet C 60 L or Ford F 60 L.

Another *beute* vehicle, this time a Ford C11ADF, a militarised station wagon powered by a V-8-cyl, 95 bhp engine. Note the two British helmets affixed below the lights of the Auto Union/Horch 901 Type 40, a V-8-cyl powered 4 x 4 medium cross-country car.

Chapter Seven
Artillery

The 10.5 cm leFH18 (*leichte Feldhaubitze* or light field howitzer) was the German Army's standard divisional light field howitzer. A 1942 U.S. intelligence document on the fighting in the Libyan Desert noted the importance of artillery: 'Guns have halted tanks and infantry; guns of all calibres—motor-drawn, self-propelled, portee, and mounted in tanks—have enabled large advances to be made by both sides.' With regard to offensive manoeuvring, Rommel noted that artillery had to be 'mobile in the highest degree, including its ammunition in large quantities'.

A battery of 10.5 cm leFH18 howitzers firing. Note the accompanying Sd.Kfz. 11. (*sonderkraftfahrzeug* – 'special motorised vehicle') half-tracks. A U.S. wartime report investigating German artillery in North Africa noted that 'although the desert is not completely flat, suitable vantage points for observation posts are never very high. This lack of height, together with the heat waves rising from the hot sand and rocks, sometimes reduces visibility in the desert. Midday is the least satisfactory period for observing fire…It has been noted that the German infantry in Libya, as elsewhere, have launched attacks for the purpose of obtaining observation posts for their artillery. In one instance such an attack was made to gain ground only three feet higher than the surrounding terrain. Similarly, German artillery officers have been known to ride on top of tanks in order to gain height for observation.'

A *schwere Feldhaubitze* 18 (15 cm sFH 18) heavy field howitzer at full recoil. Note the size of the projectile being manhandled. A multitude of factors influence the trajectory of a shell, including its weight, the force of the charge, distance to the target, wind strength and direction, air temperature and humidity, as well as the curvature of the Earth.

German 15 cm sFH 18 heavy field howitzers stirring up dust. A German artillery 'battery' usually comprised four guns, the equivalent of the British 'troop' of four to six pieces. A German 'battalion' of twelve guns was the rough equivalent of the British 'battalion' of twelve guns.

The 10 cm M 14 Feldhaubitze was the standard light field howitzer of the Austro-Hungarian Army during the First World War. It also saw service in the Wehrmacht as either 10 cm leFH 14(ö) or 10 cm leFH 315(i) and the *Regio Esercito* as the *Obice da 100/17 modello 14*.

Ex-Soviet 76.2 mm Model 1936 field guns converted for use as anti-tank guns were known as the 7.62 cm PaK 36(r). The abovementioned U.S. report cited a 'real problem which a forward artillery observer has in identifying his own bursts among the dust and heat waves when other units are also firing. Judging distance in the desert is as difficult as on the ocean. Lack of familiarity with the size and appearance of armoured vehicles at various ranges is a frequent cause for misjudging distance. The fact that the enemy opens fire does not inevitably mean that the enemy is within range, for he can misjudge distance also.'

The 10.5 cm leFH18 howitzer, introduced into Wehrmacht service in July 1935, performed well as the supporting arm of German armoured divisions.

German 5 cm Pak 38 anti-tank gun and crew. A U.S. intelligence report on German tactics in North Africa during the 26 May 1942 offensive noted: 'The enemy was quick to cover his front with antitank guns when tanks were brought to a standstill or stopped to refuel, and to protect his flanks at all times with an antitank screen. A threat to the enemy's flanks by British tanks was immediately met by the deployment of antitank artillery, while the enemy tanks continued their movement.'

An application of mud over the gun and barrel provides makeshift camouflage over the original *Dunkelgrau* colour.

Designed for loads of three tons, the *leichter Zugkraftwagen* ('light half-track vehicle') 3t Sd.Kfz.11 was manufactured by four firms from late 1937 to 1945. Vehicles with the normal *Artillerieaufbau* (normal artillery superstructure) arrangement featured seats for the driver, commander and crew of six.

The *mittlerer Zugkraftwagen* (Sd. Kfz. 7) 'medium half-track' was designed for loads up to eight tons, such as the 8.8 cm Flak gun. Some 12,000 of these vehicles were produced by several manufacturers during the war with another 30 assembled by the British Army after hostilities had ended. Note the diminutive VW-*Kübelwagen* in the foreground belonging to a *Feldpost* unit.

Shouldering ammunition in tubular steel canisters. All rounds for the 8.8 cm Flak 18/36/37 were fixed, the projectile and brass cartridge case secured, enabling them to handled, loaded and fired as a single unit. Later cartridge cases, manufactured from zinc-plated drawn steel, could fail to eject in guns hot from prolonged firing. Brass plated drawn steel was a compromise measure to overcome this problem. A wartime U.S. report noted Germany's attention to the effect of heat on weapons and munitions. All ammunition other than small arms ammunition was especially packed for the tropics and marked *Tropen* or Tp.

A 10.5 cm leFH18 howitzer towed behind a half-track, and seen firing (below). When used against tanks, it was found that 'Armour of 60-mm or less is penetrated at ranges up to 600 metres … with angle of impact from normal to 30° using charge 5 or 6. The 10.5 cm gun, model 18 penetrates all thicknesses of armour encountered at ranges up to 1,500 metres with medium charge and armour-piercing shell...'

Propaganda photographs of a Sd. Kfz. 7 half-track towing a 15 cm sFH 18 (heavy field howitzer). The tactical symbol on the half-track mudguard denotes towed howitzer battery.

The crew of a German 15 cm sFH 18 (heavy field howitzer) at rest.

Inspecting a 21 cm *Mörser* 18 (mortar) *Brummbär* ('Grizzly Bear'). The German Army's standard heavy howitzer, though classified as a mortar, could hurl a 121 kg high explosive shell up to 16.7 km (18,270 yards). Transported in two loads over long distances, the 6.51 metre gun could also be towed as a single piece, usually by a medium or heavy half-track.

Bringing a 21 cm *Mörser* 18 into action. Some 700 of these 16.4-ton guns were manufactured up until 1942 when production swung across to the 17cm *Kanone* 18, a weapon with almost twice its range.

Preparing to fire. 21 cm solid shot rounds developed for use on concrete fortifications such as the Maginot Line were pointlessly shipped to the desert, where they penetrated deep into the ground, presumably causing minimal damage.

An 8.8 cm gun firing on its carriage. During Operation Battleaxe (June, 1941), it was estimated that one British tank was knocked out for every 8.8 cm round fired. There was a British weapon in the desert that also had the potential to be used in a dual-purpose role: the QF 3.7-inch (94-mm) anti-aircraft gun. Despite its heavier weight, optics not designed for a ground attack sighting, and strain on the mounting and recuperating gear when fired at low angles, when finally utilised in an anti-tank capacity in 1942, the British weapon proved formidable against Axis armour.

German workhorse. Both Britain and Italy copied the Sd. Kfz. 7 half-track. Breda produced the vehicle under license with minor changes, known as the Tipo 61. A small number were delivered prior to the Italian armistice and a further 199 were supplied to the Wehrmacht in 1943–44. Fiat also produced a handful of similar vehicles, known as the 727. Britain's Bedford Motors produced six prototype half-tracks, codenamed 'Traclat' (Tracked Light Artillery Tractor) intended to tow 25-pounder, 17-pounder and 40-mm Bofors guns before the project was cancelled due to spiraling costs.

An 8.8 cm gun emplaced within a stone sangar. An Australian infantry officer noted the lessons his men learnt from the Germans at Tobruk in 1941: '(a) camouflage—of positions and of muzzle blast, for they have found it extremely difficult to locate his guns; (b) dummy positions—so many sangars have been constructed that we cannot in confidence assume that he is occupying one of them; (c) day discipline—practically no movement at all is seen. To the observer, the whole of the enemy territory appears unoccupied'.

The 15th Panzer Division War Diary recorded 'experience gained in the defensive battle of 15-17 June 1941': 'In order to achieve surprise, all anti-tank weapons will hold their fire until it seems likely to be successful. Even if the Pak 8.8 cm has successfully opened fire, Pak 37- and 5.0 cm guns will remain silent in order to escape the attention of enemy tanks. They will wait until the heaviest English tanks are only a few hundred metres away before opening fire with the Pzgr 40.' The *Panzergranate* 40 was a German tungsten-cored armour-piercing projectile.

3.7 cm Pak 36. Mellenthin ascribed the early successes of the DAK to three factors: 'the superior quality of our antitank guns, our systematic practice of the principle of co-operation of arms, and—last but not least—our tactical methods.' The Germans also held a distinct advantage in terms of intelligence. A comprehensive understanding of the strengths and weaknesses of every British tank in service up until June 1941 (when the Cruiser Tank Mark VI was introduced) was gleaned from combat during the French campaign. German anti-tank crews therefore appreciated the critical ranges at which to engage these vehicles, unlike British tankers in the opening rounds of the desert war who had trouble identifying German individual tank models and the optimal range at which to engage them.

The 2 cm Flak 30 was a light anti-aircraft cannon often used in a ground target role. In response to a divisional questionnaire on operations in Africa, Major Ernst-Otto Ballerstedt noted in August 1941 that 'muzzle covers that can be fired through have proved effective. Automatic weapons will, as a routine measure, be continually inspected in and out of action to ensure that they are working and ready for immediate action. Special account should be taken of the increased consumption of recoil fluid and compressed air in heavy infantry gun recuperators.

Camouflaging a heavy field howitzer, the final touches being camel-thorn bush.

Italian Artillery

The *Cannone-Mitragliera da 20/65 modello 35* (Breda) anti-aircraft gun was also used against tanks, the AP ammunition capable of penetrating 30-mm of armour at 500 metres. Note the shoulder-slung 6.5-mm *Carcano modello* 1891 cavalry carbines and M33 steel helmets.

Western Front relic: a former French *Canon de 120mm L Mle 1878 (et 1878/16) de Bange*. This 1916 model of a nineteenth-century gun featured a simplified barrel, identified by the transverse transport ring. The wheels feature *ceinture de roues* or *cingolis* (*Radgürtel* in German), literally a 'wheel belt', to remove the need for a wooden platform and to help dampen the gun's recoil. As former General Karl Boettcher recounted post-war: 'The Italian pieces [in the siege of Tobruk] were mostly obsolete, and had an insufficient range.'

Italian high explosive shell projectiles were known for their poor splintering characteristics. Australian troops noticed that Italian 'shell fragmentation seemed poor' and were astounded that 'men blown off their feet got up again'.

Rommel and his ADC, Heinz Schmidt, inspect a *Canon de 120mm L Mle 1878 (et 1878/16) de Bange*. France exported these guns to Italy in 1916 and also in 1917-18 after the Caporetto disaster which, ironically, was the battle in which Rommel won the *Pour le Mérite* for his exploits against the Italians. The German designation for the gun was: 12 cm K 371(f).

A bemused looking Rommel beside a *Cannone da 152/50* coastal gun, an Armstrong-designed artillery piece built in 1918.

Italian coastal artillery emplaced at Halfaya Pass, either a 120/45 Armstrong 1918 or a 120/45 Canet-Schneider-Armstrong 1918.

Close inspection of 120/45 Armstrong 1918 or 120/45 Canet-Schneider-Armstrong inside a sandbagged emplacement.

Although development of the Italian *Cannone da 149/35* began in 1896, the Regio Esercito still fielded 46 of these outdated guns in North Africa at the beginning of 1942.

The elderly *Cannone da 149 /35* was designed before recoil systems were incorporated into the gun carriage. As a consequence, wooden ramps and wheel belts were used to absorb the recoil energy. Although the gun needed to be relaid after each shot, it was capable of firing a 45kg projectile some 17.5 km. Mussolini's more modern heavy artillery pieces were sent to the *Corpo di Spedizione Italiano in Russia*, or CSIR, fighting on Germany's Eastern Front.

Italian Ceirano 50CMA truck armed with a 75/27 CK (*Commissione Krupp*) anti-aircraft gun *autocannone*.

Italian Ceirano 50CMA truck armed with a 75/27 CK (*Commissione Krupp*) anti-aircraft gun, the most numerous truck-mounted artillery system employed by Italy during the Second World War. The Italian weapon was based on the German 75/27 model 1906 Krupp gun. Production of the gun began prior to Italy's entry into the First World War in May 1915 on the side of the Triple Entente – Britain, France and Russia.

Italian gunners apparently receiving instructions on the firing of their *Cannone da 37/45* anti-tank gun, better known as the German 3.7 cm Pak 35/36. The *Regio Esercito* used some thirty of these German guns during the Second Italo-Abyssinian War. Italy subsequently acquired another 100 in 1940, with 87 dispatched to Libya.

A battery of Italian *Cannone da 75/46* anti-aircraft guns. Like the German 8.8 cm Flak, this gun first saw service during the Spanish Civil War. Issued with anti-aircraft and armour-piercing ammunition, the maximum rate of fire was fifteen rounds per minute.

The Italian *Cannone da 75/46* anti-aircraft gun, a replacement for the earlier 75/27 CK, was based on the Swedish 75-mm model 29 built by Bofors. The German designation for the gun was 7.5 cm Flak 264 /3 (i) or 264/4 (i). Interestingly, Krupp covertly worked with Bofors to circumvent the restrictions in German armament development imposed under the Treaty of Versailles. Krupp's new gun became the German 8.8 cm Flak/Pak.

The Italian *Cannone da 105/28* field gun was based on the French *canon de 105 mm modele Schnieder* (also known as the L 13 S) with an improved traverse mechanism. Produced from 1914 to 1919, the gun was modified for high speed towing on desert terrain in 1938 with the addition of a modified brake system, a redesigned tow hook and semi-pneumatic Celerflex tyres. It was issued with high explosive, armour-piercing and smoke projectiles.

Heavily damaged *Obice da 100/17 modello 14.*

The Italian *Cannone da 65/17 modello 13* was conceived as a pack weapon for mountain artillery in 1902 and adopted in 1913. Its limited elevation, however, hampered its use in alpine regions. Production was resumed in 1937 to replace pieces lost in the fighting in Spain and Abyssinia.

The *Cannone da 75/27 modello 1906*, a pre-1914 German Krupp design, was produced by Italian arsenals at Naples and Torino. Approximately 1,700 of these guns were still in service when Italy entered the Second World War in June 1940. Note the addition of the pressed steel wheels in place of the older wooden spoked wheels. Some DAK field batteries were also issued with this gun as a stopgap measure until sufficient German weapons arrived. The British considered the gun to be hampered by: '(1) light hitting power; (2) poor fragmentation effect; (3) at ranges above 6,600 yards, it is necessary to use a false angle of sight, slope the platform, and dig a hole for the trail.'

Two *Cannone da 75/27 modello 1906* emplaced in stone sangars.

A *Cannone da 75/27 modello 1906* in a circular sand-bagged firing pit. A circular firing platform, similar to that used by the British 25-pounder, was adopted for use in 1943, providing the obsolete gun with full 360° traverse.

The gun carriage of a *Cannone da 152/37* towed by a Breda 32 heavy tractor. This Škoda-built gun originally saw service in the Austro-Hungarian Empire where it was known as the 15 cm *Autokanone M. 15/16*. Broken down into two loads, a second tractor would tow the 9,000 kg barrel. Italy entered the Second World War with twenty-nine of these guns; by September 1942 only one four-gun battery was operational in North Africa.

Disappointed with the performance of the Krupp 75/25 gun in terms of limited traverse and elevation plus the difficulty in moving it over rough terrain, the *Regio Esercito* purchased a similar calibre French gun by Déport, designated the *Cannone da 75/27 modello 11*.

This *Cannone da 65/17 modello 13* with shield was most likely photographed in an emplacement at Tobruk. Flush with the ground, the concrete Italian emplacements impressed Rommel and influenced the design of the later German 'Tobruk' pits constructed along Hitler's Atlantic wall.

The *Regio Esercito* obtained a large number of 8-mm Austrian *Schwarzlose Model 07/12* machine guns as part of reparations at the end of the First World War. Production of this belt-fed, water-cooled machine gun began in 1905 at *Österreichische Waffenfabrik Gesellschaft*, Steyr, Austria.

Axis ordnance depot at Bardia. Italian guns include the *Cannone da 75/27* and two *Cannone da 105/28* field guns with curved shields near the motorcycle.

In the foreground a *Cannone da 105/28* field gun; in the rear a *Cannone da 75/46* anti-aircraft gun.

The Cannone da 47/32, a 47-mm infantry and anti-tank gun produced under license from the Austrian firm Böhler, was introduced in 1935. Capable of firing both HE and AP projectiles, the gun lacked a protective shield and was unable to be towed behind a truck.

A series of images shows Italian *Bersaglieri* firing a *Cannone da 47/32* from a Lancia Ro NM truck

Chapter Eight
Für Deutschland

A 15 cm sFH 18 gun frames a desert cemetery. While German other ranks venerated their commanding officer, Rommel's senior officers regularly came into conflict with him. According to one DAK company commander: 'We were inflamed with a burning hatred for Rommel when he made us pay for his blind judgement again and again due to his inflexible stubbornness. He sacrificed thousands of lives and irreplaceable material in boundless brutality to his personal ambition for no good reason or need. He took us into situations that often threatened the survival of the entire *Afrikakorps*. He used his authority in an unfair, shameful manner when he demoted responsible men who dared to raise their voices...often only to give well intentioned warnings and advice.'

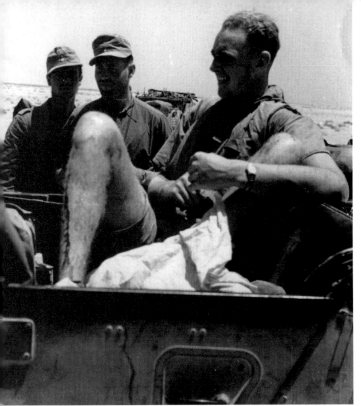

Helped by his comrades, a soldier with a leg injury is examined. Such wounds quickly deteriorated into tropical ulcers in the desert environment; 'At an early stage we had found that minor injuries, which would receive no attention in Europe, in North Africa often took a long time to heel and usually festered.'

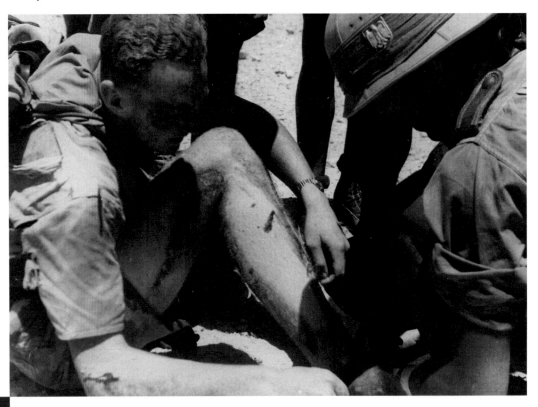

Field cemetery beside a Fascist monumental arch outside Fort Capuzzo on the Sollum Road.

Note the Sd.Ah.116 flatbed trailer, built to carry tanks up to 22/23 tons, hauling a Pz.Kpfw. III.

Empty shell cases and a *Tropenhelm* (tropical helmet) decorate a German grave.

Rommel (right) and *Leutnant* Alfred-Ingemar Berndt (*Ordonnanzoffizier Kommandierender General Panzergruppe Afrika*) pay a visit to a cemetery. Berndt wrote to Rommel's wife in August 1942 informing her about the marshal's deteriorating health: 'Your husband has now been nineteen months in Africa, which is longer than any other officer over forty has stood it so far…an astonishing feat…All this has, in the nature of things, not failed to leave its mark, and thus, in addition to all the symptoms of a heavy cold and the digestive disturbances typical of Africa, he has recently shown signs of exhaustion which have caused great anxiety to all of us who were aware of it.'

German fallen. The heavy losses suffered at Tobruk stirred up painful memories for Kirchheim: 'I do not like to be reminded of that time, because so much blood was needlessly shed.' It should also be remembered that Rommel's 7th Panzer Division suffered the highest casualty rate of any German formation during the French campaign in its dash to the English Channel.

Aerial view of the cemetery in front of the former Italian road maintenance depot, and one-time headquarters for Rommel, situated thirty-one kilometres west of Tobruk on the *Via Balbia*. These graves were exhumed in the early 1950s after the Tobruk *Soldatenfriedhof* (War Cemetery) was built.

Für Deutschland, read this grave belonging to members of the *Panzerjäger Abteilung 33* killed on 16 April 1941 at Sollum, including: *Unteroffizier* Gerhard Friedrich Ketterer, *Unteroffizier* Friedrich Heinrich Jakob, *Unteroffizier* Christoph Husemann, *Obergefreiter* Franz Gerstner, *Schütze* Karl Trabold, *Schütze* Julius Schlemmer, *Gefreiter* Hellmuth Spiess, *Schütze* Karl Kiess and *Schütze* Peter Kreuter. All the men are today buried at Tobruk.

German situation map dated 1 September 1942 showing *Alexandrien* (Alexandria) and how close Rommel came to reaching the Nile. The battles fought at El Alamein marked a turning point of the North African Campaign, and the first major irreversible German defeat of the war. Unable to push through the Allied line at Alam el Halfa (southeast of El Alamein) through a fatal combination of a chronic fuel shortage, vast minefields to negotiate and General Bernard Montgomery's devastating dominance in armour and air power, Rommel went on the defensive and prepared for a new British offensive. He had hoped to resume the offensive before the British could reorganise, but his precious supplies, especially fuel, were being lost at sea through a resurgent Malta and the unremitting attention by Desert Air Force on Axis supply lines emanating from Tripoli, Benghazi, Tobruk, Bardia and Mersa Matruh. Montgomery's desert offensive began on the night of 23 October 1942 with a massive artillery barrage by 1,900 heavy guns. His well-trained force of 230,000 troops, comprising British, Australian, New Zealanders, Free French, Indian and South African troops, faced a weary Axis army of some 50,000 Germans and 54,000 Italians. Montgomery's armoured superiority—1,440 tanks to 540--was equalled in the air with 1,500 aircraft to 350. Despite the overwhelming disparity in men and machines, a week of fierce fighting developed. Rommel's attention was firmly fixed on overcoming the Ninth Australian Division, his nemesis from 1941, but it was British armour that struck a decisive blow to his southern flank. It was a battle, Rommel observed, that 'turned the tide of war against us and, in fact, probably represented the turning point of the whole vast struggle. The conditions under which my gallant troops entered the battle were so disheartening that there was practically no hope of our coming out of it victorious'. Suffering crippling losses, Rommel ordered a general withdrawal on 2 November 1942.

Bibliography

U.S. Army Military History Institute, Carlisle, Pennsylvania.

MS # D-045 The Role of Artillery in the Siege of Tobruk.

MS # D-0424 Command Techniques Employed by Feldmarschall Rommel in Africa by Generalleutnant Alfred Gause.

Supplement to MS # D-024. D-084, Supplement to 'Reasons for Rommel's Success in Africa, 1941-42.' By Generalmajor Friedrich von Mellenthin; 5 pp; 1947.

MS # D-213 The Siege of Tobruch.

MS # D-214 Advance Towards Tobruk by the Italian Division 'Brescia' April 1941.

MS # P-130 Camouflage.

Artillery in the Desert, Military Intelligence Service, Special Series No. 6, November 1942.

P-129 German experiences in Desert Warfare During World War II—supplement by Generalleutnant Fritz Bayerlein and Dr Sigismund Kienow.

P-108, Collaboration Between Germany and her Allies during World War II, Part I.

D-217, Italo-German Cooperation in Italian North Africa.

T-3 North African Campaign, Vol. 1 & 2.

Published Sources

Ball, S. *Alamein: Great Battles*. Oxford, 2016

Battistelli, P.P. *Erwin Rommel*. Oxford, 2010.

---- *Rommel's Afrika Korps: Tobruk to El Alamein*. Oxford, 2006.

Beckett, I.F.W. *Rommel- A Reappraisal*. Barnsley, 2013.

Butler, D.A. *Field Marshal: The Life and Death of Erwin Rommel*. Havertown [Pennsylvania], 2015

Behrendt, H-O. *Rommel's Intelligence in the Desert Campaign*. London, 1985.

Brighton, T. *Masters of Battle: Monty, Patton and Rommel at War*. London, 2008.

Caddick-Adams, P. *Monty and Rommel: Parallel Lives*. London, 2012.

Carruthers, B. *The Panzer III*. Barnsley, 2013.

Carver, M. *Tobruk*. London, 1964.

Citino, R.M. *Death of the Wehrmacht: The German Campaigns of 1942*. Lawrence [Kansas], 2011.

Corrigan, G. *Blood, Sweat and Arrogance: The Myths of Churchill's War*. London, 2006.

Davis, G. *In My Father's Footsteps: With the 53rd Welsh Division from Normandy to Hamburg*. Barnsley, 2015.

Fennell, J. *Combat and Morale in the North African Campaign*. Cambridge, 2011.

Finazzer E. and R.A. Riccio. *Italian Artillery of WWII*. Poland, 2015.

Fletcher, D. *British Light Tanks 1927-45: Marks I-VI*. Oxford, 2014.

_ _ _ *Matilda Infantry Tank 1938–45*. Oxford, 1994.

Forty, G. *Afrika Korps at War Vol 1: The Road to Alexandria*. New York, 1978.

_ _ _ *Afrika Korps at War Vol 2: The Long Road Back*. New York, 1979.

Gander, T. *German 88: The Most Famous Gun of the Second World War*. Barnsley, 2009.

Hamilton, N. *Commander in Chief: FDR's Battle with Churchill, 1943*. Boston, 2016.

Hart, P. *The South Notts Hussars: The Western Desert, 1940-1942*. Barnsley, 2011.

Hartman, B. *Panzers in the Sand: The History of Panzer-Regiment 5, 1935-41* (Volume 1). Barnsley, 2010.

_ _ _ *Panzers in the Sand: The History of Panzer-Regiment 5, 1942-45* (Volume 2). Barnsley, 2011.

Henry, C. *The 25-Pounder Field Gun, 1939-72*. Oxford, 2002.

Herf, J. *Nazi Propaganda for the Arab World*. New Haven, 2009.

Hogg, I. *German Artillery of World War Two*. London, 1997.

Holland, J. *The War in the West - A New History: Volume 1: Germany Ascendant 1939-1941*. London, 2015.

Irving, D. *The Trail of the Fox*. Hertfordshire, 1977.

Jentz, T. Tank *Combat in North Africa: The Opening Rounds, Operations Sonnenblume, Brevity, Skorpion and Battleaxe February 1941 - June 1941*. Atglen, 1998.

Jowett, P.S. *The Italian Army 1940-45 (1): Europe 1940-43*. Oxford, 2002.

Kesselring, A. *The Memoirs of Field-Marshal Kesselring*. London, 1974.

Kurowski, F. *Knight's Cross Holders of the Afrikakorps*. Atglen [Pennsylvania], 1996.

Kitchen, M. *Rommel's Desert War*. Cambridge, 2009.

Levine, A.J. *The War Against Rommel's Supply Lines 1942-1943*. Westport, 1999.

Lewin, R. *The Life and Death of the Afrika Korps*. London 1977.

Liddell Hart, B.H., ed. *The Rommel Papers*. London, 1953.

Longerich, P. *Goebbels*. New York, 2015.

McNab, C. *Hitler's Armies: A history of the German War Machine 1939–45*. 2011. Oxford, 2011.

Mitcham, S.W. *Rommel's Lieutenants: The Men Who Served the Desert Fox, France, 1940*. Mechanicsburg, 2009.

Mitcham, S.W. *Rommel's Desert Commanders: The Men Who Served the Desert Fox, North Africa*. Mechanicsburg, 2008.

Mitchelhill-Green, D. *Tobruk 1942*, Stroud, 2016.

Olive, M. *Steel Thunder on the Eastern Front: German and Russian Artillery in WWII*. Mechanicsburg, 2014.

Pallud, J.P. *The Desert War: Then and Now*. London, 2013.

Rau, P. *Our Nazis: Representations of Fascism in Contemporary Literature and Film*. Edinburgh, 2013.

Reuth, R.G. *Rommel: The End of the Legend*. London, 2010.

Rubin, S. & Schwanitz, W.G. *Nazis, Islamists, and the Making of the Modern Middle East*. New Haven, 2014.

Schmidt, H.W. *With Rommel in the Desert*. London, 1951.

Schraepler, H.A. *At Rommel's Side: The Lost Letters of Han Joachim Schraepler*, London, 2009.

Schreiber, G. et al. *Germany and the Second World War, Volume III: The Mediterranean, South-east Europe, and North Africa 1939-1941*. Oxford, 1995.

Showalter, D. *Patton and Rommel: Men of War in the Twentieth Century*. Berkley, 2005.

Stockings, C. *Bardia: Myth, Reality and the Heirs of Anzac*. Sydney, 2010.

Taylor, B. *Volkswagen Military Vehicles of the Third Reich: An Illustrated History*. Boulder, 2004.

Turner, H.A. *General Motors and the Nazis: The Struggle for Control of Opel, Europe's Biggest Carmaker*. New Haven, 2005.

van Creveld, M. *Supplying War: Logistics from Wallenstein to Patton*. New York, 1980.

Vanderveen, B.H. *Historic Military Vehicles Directory*. London, 1989.

Von Luck, H. *Panzer Commander: The Memoirs of Colonel Hans von Luck*. New York, 1989.

Von Mellenthin, F. W. *Panzer Battles*. New York, 1956.

Westphal, S. *The German Army in the West*. London, 1951.

Wilmot, C. *Tobruk 1941*, Sydney, 1944.

Zabecki, D. T. *Chief of Staff, Vol. 2: The Principal Officers Behind History's Great Commanders, World War II to Korea and Vietnam*. Annapolis, 2013.

Periodicals

Time, Volume 57, 22 January 1951.